p. 91 -

SHOW ME
YOUR WAY

SHOW ME YOUR WAY

The Complete Guide to Exploring Interfaith Spiritual Direction

HOWARD A. ADDISON

Walking Together, Finding the Way

SKYLIGHT PATHS Publishing
Woodstock, Vermont

*Show Me Your Way: The Complete Guide to Exploring
Interfaith Spiritual Direction*

Library of Congress Cataloging-in-Publication Data
Addison, Howard A., 1950–
Show me your way : the complete guide to exploring interfaith
spiritual direction / by Howard A. Addison.
p.   cm.
Includes bibliographical references (p.).
ISBN 1-893361-12-8
1. Spiritual direction. 2. Religious pluralism. I. Title.

BL624 .A33 2000
291.6'1—dc21   00-026547

10 9 8 7 6 5 4 3 2 1

Manufactured in the United States of America
Jacket design by Drena Fagen
Text design by Susan Ramundo

Published by SkyLight Paths Publishing
A Division of LongHill Partners, Inc.
Sunset Farm Offices, Route 4, P.O. Box 237
Woodstock, VT 05091
Tel: (802) 457-4000   Fax: (802) 457-4004
www.skylightpaths.com

To Sister Barbara

"Her mouth opens with wisdom;
Kind guidance is upon her tongue."
—Proverbs 31:26

Contents

ACKNOWLEDGMENTS

The Hebrew name for one who is Jewish is *Yehudi* or *Yehudiah*. These male and female terms are both derived from the same root as the word *todah,* thanks. Since my own faith places gratefulness at the core of our spiritual identity, let me take this opportunity to thank those whose guidance and support have made this book possible.

At a critical point in my past I attended two seminars sponsored by the Alban Institute, an interfaith center located in the Washington, D.C., area. There I was introduced to both spiritual direction and the Enneagram system of personality type. These two disciplines are now among the most crucial supports to my spiritual and professional life. I will always be grateful to Reverend Roy Oswald, an Alban senior consultant, for those seminars and his teaching.

The writings and spirit of the Reverend Dr. Tilden Edwards and Sister Rose Mary Dougherty inform almost every page of this book. It has been a privilege to study with them at the Shalem Institute. Both this text and I are richer for their continued friendship and guidance.

Speaking of guidance, since 1995 I have been fortunate to have had two wonderful spiritual directors. Sister Elizabeth Hilman of the Cenacle House in Lantana, Florida, helped make my academic interest in the inner life become an everyday reality. Sister Barbara Whittemore is the epitome of a spiritual friend. Our monthly sessions at the Cenacle House in Highland Park, New Jersey, bring insight and depth to moments of exaltation and help illumine even the darkest nights of the soul.

Let me thank the staff of SkyLight Paths for their support. Its publisher, Stuart Matlins, took a chance on me some years back when I was a fledgling author. Jon Sweeney, the associate publisher, was the first to suggest the topic for this book. I am also grateful to Sandra Korinchak, vice president of editorial operations, and to my editor, Dave O'Neal who has a wonderful feel for both the world of literature and the world of religious faith.

This book would not have come to fruition without the sharing and courage of those who agreed to be interviewed for its pages. Special thanks to Dr. Laleh Bakhtiar of Kazi Books in Chicago, Dr. Beatrice Bruteau, and Claude d'Estrée, who served as expert resources in the philosophy and practice of Islam, Hinduism, and Buddhism respectively.

Finally I must thank two people: Donna, my friend and coworker, whose research assistance, editorial suggestions, encouragement, and manuscript preparation are absolutely invaluable; and Adina, whose enthusiasm and faith in this project rivaled and sometimes even exceeded my own.

—HOWARD A. ADDISON
March 2000

PREFACE

It was in the summer of 1998, at the New Age International Trade Show in Denver, that Jon Sweeney, associate publisher of SkyLight Paths Publishing, suggested that I write a book on interfaith spiritual direction. Jon knew that I had been in spiritual direction for some time with an order of Catholic sisters, and he wondered just how prevalent the practice of interfaith spiritual direction might be. He asked me to think about it.

Well, I did, for three months, until I decided to go ahead with the research and writing that have led to this book.

I would be less than candid if I didn't admit to having some qualms about the project. In my religious practice and in my heart I am something of a traditionalist. I have spent much of my life trying to present Judaism in a meaningful way, trying to encourage Jews to remain Jews and become more committedly so. Claude d'Estrée, a Buddhist of Russian Orthodox descent who works with people of all backgrounds as an interfaith spiritual guide, told me he feels that ninety percent of all people actually belong in the faith of their birth. I pretty much agree with his assessment and hope that individuals are able to find the inspiration and solace they need within their own traditions.

As I'll try to show in the pages that follow, there is much to be gained when people of faith share perspectives with each other while respecting each other's boundaries. However, in the free religious marketplace of melting-pot America there are also certain hazards: In the race for market share and profits, modern commercialism tends to trivialize the symbols and observances that historically have differentiated the great religions. Holiday greeting cards with Christmas trees and menorahs framing the caption "Happy Whatever" do violence to two sacred traditions and their respective messages.

Another danger is the perpetration of fraud. In their attempt to gain converts, certain missionary groups are not above hijacking the religious language and observances of another faith. Rather than openly publicize their own message, missionaries sometimes wrap their beliefs in the celebrations, music, and holy days of the tradition whose members they are targeting so as to lure the unsuspecting. The Bill of Rights does guarantee freedom of religion and the right to choose among faiths. However, we should be able to make informed choices based on honest presentations.

On a more personal note I wondered if the appearance of this book might undermine other aspects of my work. For the last several years I have been slowly trying to introduce aspects of contemplative spirituality into mainstream Jewish denominational life. Despite my own commitment to traditional observance and my investigation of the legitimate biblical and kabbalistic roots of such practices, I feared the publication of this book might raise further suspicion. After all, if Rabbi Addison is receiving spiritual guidance from nuns, how can these innovations be genuinely Jewish?

But as the weeks went by I became more convinced that this was a text I had to write. As I will describe in Chapter 4, my upbringing on Chicago's South Side was intensely Jewish. However, in a real sense, that Jewish identity was shaped by my relationship to another tradition—Christianity. Since my parents were not yet observant during my earliest years, I did not actually realize that I was Jewish until I was five. It was then that I asked my parents why I wasn't attending kindergarten at Saint Felicity's with the other kids on my block. I think it was that question as much as any other factor that first galvanized the Addisons' efforts to live more fully as Jews.

During my adult years, my doctoral studies at the Jesuit-sponsored Fordham University and at the United Church of Christ's Chicago Theological Seminary enriched my understanding not only of philosophy and religion but of Judaism as well. They gave me a new set of interpretive tools by which to evaluate and internalize the lessons I had learned at the Jewish Theological Seminary.

Seminars sponsored by the Alban Institute and the Shalem Institute, two interdenominational Christian centers near Washington, D.C., deepened my appreciation of spiritual inwardness and inspired me to search for similar faith expressions within historic Judaism. These seminars also introduced me to two disciplines that have become vital to my own spiritual journey. One is the Enneagram system of personality type, about which I wrote my earlier book, *The Enneagram and Kabbalah: Reading Your Soul* (Jewish Lights, 1998). The other is the life-changing counsel that I derived from spiritual guidance, which will be discussed in the pages ahead.

A few words about terminology: There are a variety of words used to describe spiritual direction and those who participate in it. The enterprise itself has been called *spiritual direction, guidance, companioning,* and *friendship.* Historically these have represented a continuum of authority. Direction has been the most prescriptive and least egalitarian, bordering on the master/disciple relationship. Spiritual guidance reflects a difference of experience more than of authority—a veteran traveler along the spiritual path would use his or her acquired insights to help point the way for relative newcomers. Companioning and friendship indicate greater mutuality, that of equals offering counsel and support to each other.

In this text *direction* and *guidance,* and *director* and *guide* will be used interchangeably for stylistic clarity. The terms *companion* and *friend* will be reserved for the mutual counsel of peers.

The term *seeker(s)* will be used in two different ways. One will reflect the general sense of those who are searching for meaning and exploring the wisdom of different traditions as part of their quest. The other, more technical usage will be in reference to those who have sought out spiritual direction and are in a guidance relationship. I use *seeker* in this sense because terms like *directee* and *advisee* are too clumsy, and *companion* or *friend* imply the mutuality of an equal peer relationship. I have tried to make clear which sense of the term *seeker* is intended by the context in which the word appears.

The personal testimonies in this book come from a variety of sources. Some reflect my own experiences in spiritual direction. Other accounts were related to me in the course of interviews conducted as part of my research.

The responses of various interfaith spiritual directors and seekers to questions I asked provided a third source. Questions included the following:

For Seekers
1. What life circumstances led you to seek spiritual direction?
2. What motivated you to seek spiritual direction outside your own tradition?
3. What new insights about faith and God's working in your life have you derived?
4. Have your experiences given you a new perspective on aspects of your own tradition?
5. Have you or anyone else you know had a negative experience resulting from interfaith spiritual direction?
6. What would you advise someone considering interfaith spiritual direction about its benefits and drawbacks?

For Spiritual Directors
1. How do the motivations and circumstances of seekers coming to you from another faith differ from those of seekers from your own faith? In what ways are they the same?
2. How do you discern whether to enter into a relationship of spiritual guidance with a seeker? What additional factors do you consider when an applicant is of a different faith?
3. How does the guidance you offer to someone of another faith differ from what you offer to someone of your own?

4. How have your perceptions or experiences of a seeker's faith influenced the direction you offered?
5. How has the experience of guiding someone from another faith affected or changed you?
6. Can you cite any vignettes from your tradition in which members of other faiths came to consult a spiritual guide from yours?
7. Has your experience with interfaith spiritual direction led you to any reflections about religious unity and diversity as we begin the next millennium?

To preserve a sense of privacy, I have, in most cases, only recorded the first names of those who responded by questionnaire or interview. Unattributed statements and vignettes were either contributed anonymously or represent a desire of the respondent to preserve greater confidentiality.

The title of this book is taken from the twenty-fifth Psalm:

Show me Your Way O Lord
Teach me Your path
Guide me in Your truth
And instruct me,
For You are God, my Salvation
For You I yearn all the day.

From my experience, when people of different traditions show each other their way, with humility and respect for each other's boundaries, their teachings can more fully reveal the path to God. It is my prayer that through such guidance we might gain glimpses of God's truth and experience that taste of salvation for which we, along with the psalmist, fervently yearn.

Part One

THE SEARCH

1

BREWING SPIRITS: A HASIDIC TALE

Long ago in a small Eastern European village there lived a Jew named Yankel. Month after month he eked out a meager living, earning barely enough to keep his family alive. Frustrated by his poverty, Yankel began to dream of a richer, fuller life. So he hatched a plan.

Each day he asked a different friend for suggestions concerning how he might find an occupation that would bring him the riches he so fervently desired. Soon a consensus developed. Mead is not only a fine drink, claimed his friends, but a great way to make a living. After all, isn't mead served at every bar mitzvah, wedding, and festive event? Weary travelers love to wet their throats with mead after a long, hot journey. Workmen, spent from a hard day, forget their toils by lifting a frothy mug in toast to each other. With such a market for spirits who could go wrong?

So Yankel began to learn all he could about mead. He inquired of the local innkeepers. He read what he could. Daily he practiced the distilling arts. Finally, when he thought he was ready, Yankel brewed his first batch of mead. Calling his friends together, he poured each a glass and bid them to drink to his success. Glancing around, Yankel noticed strained looks as his friends drank. He lifted his own mug and found that the spirits tasted flat, almost bitter—not what he had expected at all.

Dejected but not defeated, Yankel remembered that in the city of Kiev there lived a great brewmaster whose reputation was known far and wide. Packing up his belongings in a small bag, Yankel kissed his family good-bye and hurried off to Kiev. Upon reaching the city he began to inquire where the brewmaster might be found. After searching high and low, a tired Yankel finally came upon his mentor-to-be.

Over the course of several days Yankel reviewed his ingredients and procedures with the brewer.

"Are you sure you used the right proportions?" asked the brewmaster.

"Absolutely," replied Yankel.

"Well, I'm not really sure what happened."

"Do you mean I came all this way for nothing?" Yankel cried.

"Not necessarily," said the brewmaster as he reached into a sack. Slowly he extracted an amber jar. "While not everything can be revealed through words, might you have something like this?"

Immediately Yankel realized why he had been led to Kiev. He thanked the brewmaster, grabbed his belongings, and headed home. No sooner did he arrive than he began to root through his pantry. There on a low shelf was a small jar of honey. Yankel scooped up the jar and rushed off to make a fresh batch of mead.

When the spirits were ready Yankel again summoned his friends. This time smiles and approval came forth as Yankel and company drained their mugs. From that day forward Yankel's mead delighted not only the palates of customers from near and far, it delighted his own palate as well.[1]

When first reading this Hasidic tale you might be struck by the simplicity of its message: In the midst of our need, the ingredients for fulfillment are right at hand. Sweetness is no further away than our own pantry. Perseverance and the encouragement of a supportive community can spur us along as we seek to enrich our lives and the lives of others.

However, a closer reading of this story yields some interesting observations. While the honey was always sitting on his shelf, Yankel had no idea of its importance. It was his sense of dissatisfaction that started Yankel on a journey of discovery that ultimately led back to his own pantry. Only by going to Kiev and encountering the brewmaster did Yankel even become aware of where to look. Guided by their interaction, Yankel gained the insight to find the missing ingredient and claim the sweetness that had always been his.

Interestingly enough the brewmaster never prescribed a remedy to cure the bitterness of Yankel's mead. Instead he had Yankel review each of his steps and then held an object lesson before him, leading Yankel to his own realizations. In the end Yankel himself became an accomplished brewer. His efforts not only brought riches and personal fulfillment, but also satisfaction and a quenching of thirst for those around him.

As one millennium gives way to the next many of us can identify with Yankel. Spiritually we, too, yearn for richer, fuller lives. We might investigate, gain counsel and a sense of community from those around us while drawing upon the resources at hand. Yet at times, despite the best efforts, our home brew can seem flat, leaving our spirits unsatisfied, leaving some of us with a bitter aftertaste.

Yankel's story could have had different endings. He might have stayed in Kiev, leaving family and friends behind to make a new home while apprenticing himself to the brewer. Alternately he could have taken to the road again, traveling from one brewmaster to another in a continuing search for the perfect recipe. Instead Yankel drew upon guidance from this mentor beyond home to return, recombine his own ingredients with an extra flavoring he already had, and thus brew more satisfying spirits for himself and his fellows.

In our times there are many who feel they can only quench their spiritual thirst by drinking from wellsprings of various traditions. Some formally adopt a different faith. Others travel a continuing path seeking wisdom from a variety of teachings and teachers. However, given today's uniquely diverse religious climate, another option exists to an extent previously unknown in world history. That option is interfaith spiritual direction. The interaction of your own knowledge and longings with the insights of a guide from beyond your religious home can reveal new realms of spiritual truth as you embark on a wide-ranging journey of faith. You, too, may discover a sweetness of spirit—sweetness waiting to be uncovered within your own soul and, perhaps, sweetness within your own heritage that you didn't even know or recall was there.

2

SEEKERS

SARAH'S STORY

Sarah was born into a Roman Catholic family. Although her father, an accomplished physicist, professed to be an agnostic, the rhythms of their family life were those of the Catholic liturgical year. Devotions, holy days, attention to the sacraments, and regular church attendance were all imperatives of the household and staples of Sarah's life.

> As a young girl my heart was filled with Jesus. My favorite movie was *The Greatest Story Ever Told*, and its scenes would play over and over in my mind. So each morning during Lent I'd get up early, go to Mass, and only then join the other thirteen-year-olds to go to school.

A dilemma confronted Sarah as she reached her later high school years. Her longing for intense religious experience continued to grow but she didn't want to enter a convent, take vows, and become a nun. Because she despaired of finding the spiritual succor she craved as a Catholic laywoman, Sarah began to explore different philosophies and faith traditions. For her needs she found Protestantism lacking. Her search finally took her to a Buddhist temple and her first exposure to an Asian spiritual tradition.

Moved by the message and practices of Paramahansa Yogananda (d. 1952), an Indian master who taught extensively in the West, she became an initiate of his Self-Realization Fellowship.[1] Yet one night Sarah had a troubling dream. She envisioned Yogananda seated on a stage before her. Calmly he looked at her and said, "Sarah, I'm not your teacher." Although she maintains her respect for Yogananda's teachings even to this day, Sarah left the SRF to continue her search.

With far less respect and much greater cynicism, Sarah describes her experiences with a variety of gurus in Philadelphia during the 1970s:

> It was as if they were running a franchise business. They divided the territory among themselves with every guru having his own domain. From time to time they would call upon each other. The disciples would prepare the meals and then feel blessed if they were given leftovers from the masters' plates. The visiting guru would lavishly extol his host as the disciples listened with rapt attention. This confirmed their allegiance and belief in the spiritual renown of their teacher. After all, his soul must shine if Guru X just praised him so.

If Sarah is skeptical about the self-congratulatory practices of the "guru cartel," she expresses nothing but disdain for their sexual adventures:

Not only did they have affairs with their disciples; these young women were convinced that they, as disciples, should be proud of it. When I asked them if they realized what they were doing, the dismissive response was, "You wouldn't understand. This is a special bonding between the master's spirit and mine." Once, before I knew such things were going on, I found myself alone in a room with one of these gurus. Without a second thought he said, "You can kiss me all you want. After all, I am an idol of the divine." I didn't know what to think or what to say, but I stayed right where I was.

For two years Sarah dropped out of the spirituality scene completely. Given what she had witnessed she decided to be guru to herself. However, as the months passed, her despair grew as she realized that she needed a true guide. A diminutive Sufi from Sri Lanka, Bawa Muhaiyaddeen, had settled in Philadelphia. With a doubting mind Sarah went to meet this eclectic teacher of Islam in 1975.

I was prepared to question anything he said that made me suspicious, that I didn't understand; but at first when I entered the crowded room I only noticed his eyes. He looked at you without distraction or pretense and I knew I could look into those eyes as long and as deeply as I cared to. I knew that I had never previously met anyone like this.

During a question-and-answer session following his address, I asked, "Bawa, how do you know a true teacher?"

"When you find a true teacher it is like looking into a mirror. When you look into his eyes you will see yourself revealed."

I was so moved by these simple words that I returned for a private meeting the next day.

Bawa offered no magical mantras and made no claims of spiritual powers. But those deep eyes and that sincere offer to help confirmed that here was the spiritual guide Sarah's dreams had envisioned days and weeks before.

GOING SHOPPING

Perhaps the most unusual thing about Sarah's story is that in America today it's not unusual at all. The Dalai Lama has referred to our country as a "spiritual supermarket,"[2] and it would be hard to find a more apt description.

A whole potpourri of Eastern and Western faiths, New Age beliefs, and mystical practices from cultures that span all of space and time are there for the picking. You can pluck them off the Internet, cable TV, bookstore shelves, religious institutions, retreat houses, and centers throughout the land. Religious book sales leaped from $519 million in 1992 to $982 million in 1997.[3] The New York Open Center drew 25,000 people in 1998 to a whole range of workshops in kabbalah, mystical Christianity, yoga, and Buddhism, as well as art, music, holistic health, and sexuality.[4]

America's new eclectic religious attitude is strikingly revealed in a survey that tracked a large number of adults who had been confirmed in a variety of churches during the 1960s. Twenty years later only one-third had remained within their own denomination. While most occasionally participated in organized religion, eight out of ten thought one's religious beliefs should be arrived at independently of any religious organization. Seven out of ten felt that all religions were equally good ways to find ultimate truth.[5] It is, therefore, little wonder that some Americans now blend their own mix of traditions, calling

themselves "Episcopalian-practicing non-Jew," or "Men-
nonite-Unitarian Universalist Zen Meditator," or the in-
creasingly popular "Jewish Buddhist" or JewBu for short.[6]

HISTORICAL PRECEDENTS
AND THE UNPRECEDENTED

Cultural history is actually replete with examples of borrowings among faith traditions. In the West, *El,* used by
the Hebrew Bible when referring to the God of Israel, was
initially the name of a high deity of the Canaanite pan-
theon.[7] Jesus' two great commands in Matthew 22:34–40,
"You shall love the Lord your God" and "Love your neigh-
bor as yourself," are taken straight from Deuteronomy 6:5
and Leviticus 19:18. The Holy Koran's tale of Abraham
taking his son to be sacrificed in sura 37:99–111 echoes
the story of Abraham, Isaac, and Mount Moriah in
Genesis 22.

In Asia certain Jain parables are also found in
Hindu tradition.[8] Hinduism and Buddhism share terms
like *dharma* and *karma* and both incorporated and adapt-
ed aspects of earlier cults from the Ganges valley.[9] Zen
Buddhism might owe as much of its origins to Chinese
Taoism and Confucianism as it does to Indian teaching.[10]

These borrowings rarely went one way only, and
their patterns of interconnection are often complex. Great
flood stories cut across national boundaries, with the hero
known as Manu in India, Utnapishtim in Mesopotamia,
Xisouthros in Greece, and Noah in ancient Israel.[11] While
the New Testament and the Holy Koran owe a debt to the
Hebrew Bible, the Jewish mystical tradition, kabbalah, is
thought by some to have drawn upon early Christian
asceticism and the Sufism of Islam.[12]

One intriguing tale revolves around the prophecies of latter Isaiah (Isaiah 40–66). Because these verses often evoke the image of a suffering God ("In all their afflictions God was pained." 63:9), Christians identified them with the Passion and Crucifixion of Jesus. In this century the great philosopher Rabbi Abraham Joshua Heschel reclaimed these empathic images for Judaism. He spoke of God in English terms like the "God of Pathos" and the "Most Moved Mover."[13] A backlash developed in the Jewish community, with traditionalists protesting Heschel's reclamation of these metaphors as an unwarranted bridge to Christianity. One Talmudic sage reputedly tried to forbid Jewish preachers from citing latter Isaiah in their sermons because of its Christian allusions!

These examples, and countless others, indicate clearly that borrowing, mutual influence, and adaptation are part of an ongoing dynamic in the development of faith traditions. A rite, a tale, or an idea might make its way from one faith community to another either as a folk practice or in the teachings of a recognized sage. Inevitably a process of reinterpretation would begin whereby the practice, story, or concept would be "converted" from its former context into its new religion. The skipping lamb of ancient Near Eastern spring rites reappears in Judaism as the Paschal Lamb of Passover and, centuries later, would be identified by Christians as Jesus, the Lamb of God.[14]

However, it was communal authority and acceptance that ultimately validated such transformations. Borrowed folk practices needed legitimization by a community's recognized sages and elite. Conversely, transfigured concepts and ideas advanced by scholars and saints needed popular acceptance to become part of a community's living tradition.

Within polytheistic cultures people did worship more than one deity and support various shrines, but they did so according to the accepted practice of each sect. While the monotheistic religions at times used repression and war to maintain the "purity of the faith," instances of syncretism—the blending of beliefs and practices from two or more faiths—did occur.[15] However, unlike today, such blending was more communal than personal in nature and was not held out as an ideal. The book of Judges (21:25) berates as chaos that which some today extol as a virtue: "everyone doing what is right in their own eyes."

WHERE AMERICA DIFFERS

The primacy of individual choice in our current religious scene can be traced in part to traditions as old as America itself. The Bill of Rights protects not only an individual's freedom of religion, but also freedom *from* religion and, by implication, the freedom to pick and choose among religions as well. Thomas Jefferson claimed that our spirits are naturally inclined to think freely and weigh options. Therefore, our most genuine convictions can only be formed as a result of wide-ranging free exploration.[16] A host of changing conditions since the end of World War II has helped free the exercise of that personal exploration beyond anything Jefferson might have imagined two centuries ago.

Family life, once the glue that bound people to locations, traditions and each other, has undergone radical transformations. In the late 1950s the average American woman married by age twenty and bore 3.8 children. Half of all households had at least one child under eighteen and eighty-five percent of the elderly lived near a grown daughter or son. On average, city dwellers knew twenty-seven of their relatives personally and were close enough to visit most on occasion.[17]

During the last half century this familial glue has lost its hold. The birth rate has gone down while the age of marriage and rate of divorce has gone up. The ease of travel and the call of new economic opportunities have dissolved clans. People have spread across the map and relationships are currently formed on the shifting basis of consent rather than ties of kinship, family tradition, and descent. Even home, once a place where the family lived, is now more a point of departure. The ever more isolated occupants of the home now go off to their own TVs or computers, or leave in their cars to pursue separate paths.

New political, commercial, and social trends continually challenge the notion that there is but one uniform, correct way. The upheavals of the sixties undermined our belief in established institutions. Consumerism pushes us toward ever greater freedom of choice, as we select not between right and wrong, but between better and worse as determined by price and convenience. Rapid, affordable world travel, the migration of peoples and cultures from Asia, Africa, and Latin America to the U. S., and the telecommunications explosion have helped globalize almost everything. As Rodger Kamenetz, author of *The Jew in the Lotus,* stated: "We're no longer living [solely] in an Episcopal neighborhood or a Jewish neighborhood. It's easy to look over the fence and see what the other folks are doing."[18]

These factors have helped create a different, more self-directed American religious culture over the last five decades. As Robert Withnow has argued, the spirituality of the fifties was a spirituality of dwelling for residents of stable communities in surer times. It was a spirituality of social location. Your status was ascribed to membership in a group or achieved by working to attain an existing position that was there to be claimed. Security was found in known resources and shared responsibilities. People were spiritual producers, building respectable houses of worship and providing them with volunteers to staff committees and children to carry on the faith. This spirituality of dwelling, however, was also exclusive to its individual communities and was sometimes racist. It domesticated God and could venerate institutional imperatives above individual human needs. As the world grew ever less dependable, it was a spirituality whose life view and structures could not ultimately be depended upon.

This dynamic was vividly portrayed in a 1998 movie, *Pleasantville*. David and Jennifer, a brother and sister from the nineties, were magically transported into the idyllic setting of Pleasantville, a 1950s television rerun. Everything about Pleasantville seemed just right—the people were always courteous, relationships were wholesome, and no problem arose that couldn't be resolved within a half-hour. Even the high-school basketball team won all of its games. Only one problem existed—the conformity of behavior and beliefs that rendered Pleasantville pleasant also rendered its environment and residents monotonously and literally gray. As David and Jennifer questioned the territorial, intellectual, and even sexual boundaries of this perfect but uniform society, individuality and shades of color were portrayed as breaking through the black and white. Soon strife arose as those who remained gray fought to keep Pleasantville pleasant in the face of the perceived threat presented by the newly "coloreds." Slurs, family discord, violence, and a book burning all marked Pleasantville's uneasy efforts in dealing with fresh ideas and change. Beliefs and institutions that had seemed infallible required painful readjustment in the face of what was different and new.

The spirituality that has evolved since the Pleasantville fifties is more a spirituality of seeking for commuters who live between sacred spaces rather than within them. It is a spirituality of self-expression. We create our own identity; status is now negotiated from among a wide range of options.

Concerned far more with outcomes than with set group rules, it is a spirituality of consumption. Professional experts produce religious goods and services that are selected and acquired based on how individuals feel their lives will be enriched. With conditions constantly in flux, faith is no longer something we inherit but something we must strive for. We travel the globe—information pours in from across the world—and the sacred no longer seems to have one address.[19]

STEPHEN'S STORY: THE SPIRITUAL COMMUTE

No one I ever met has traveled between sacred spaces quite the way Stephen has. If spiritual trends can be captured in a single biography, that biography might well be his.

Even as a young boy, Stephen's family's home alternated between Long Island and Detroit, depending on the needs of his father's business. Although ethnically Jewish, his paternal grandparents had become Christian Scientists soon after Stephen's dad had celebrated his bar mitzvah. Stephen himself remembers his grandparents taking him to a different church each Sunday because they wanted him to gain a respect for all religions. Even though Stephen became a bar mitzvah in Detroit, he did not consider himself Jewish:

> Synagogue seemed to be a place you went once a year where the rabbi talked for four hours; you had to wear a tie and people were constantly "shushing" you. There was no spirit and no fun. . . . Sabbath observance was alien to us. It seemed reserved for the "crazy people." In Great Neck I had once seen people who would only walk and not ride in cars on Saturday. . . . If the prayers proclaimed "God is Father" then I figured this God must look something like George Washington, and I wasn't buying it . . .

Having returned to Great Neck for high school, Stephen's early teen years were spent as an atheist. While working at his school's library he began to check out books on Zen meditation and philosophy, books such as Andrew Weil's *Natural Mind,* which challenged his lack of belief. He began to consider whether all consciousness was actually one, whether there was an "I" behind the "I" of self.

A particularly disturbing dream about a fire and flower shook Stephen's sense of balance and self. Not knowing where to turn and sure that there was nothing spiritual in Judaism, he began to attend meetings of a local Nichiren Shoshu Buddhist group with a friend. Soon he started to question the entire experience.

> The group felt very proselytizing and very commercial. The focus seemed to be on bringing new people in and then getting them to buy an assortment of beads and scripture in calligraphy.
> Each week we were supposed to chant the mantra *nam-myoho-renge-kyo*. Wednesday night was testi-

mony night. The tone of the evening was bouncy, upbeat, and quite materialistic. Men and women would describe how many hours they had chanted the previous week and the resulting benefits they had derived: one million dollars, a new stereo system, or the affection of their latest love interest. Little, if any, attention seemed to be focused on the inner life.

If a dream had brought Stephen to Nichiren Buddhism, a film brought him back to Christian Science, the faith that had attracted his grandparents some decades before.

During the week of my high school graduation a few of us went to see *The Exorcist*. It scared the s— out of me. Frightened to the core, I needed to talk to someone who could give me spiritual guidance. I dismissed the notion of a rabbi with hardly a second thought. I considered calling a priest but didn't because, hey, I wasn't a Catholic.

A close friend, Tommy, directed Stephen to the local Christian Science Reading Room. There he encountered a Christian Science practitioner who spoke to him about God as Infinite Mind, healing through spirit, and Satan as a mere error in our way of thinking.

The practitioner told me to read the writings of their founder, Mary Baker Eddy. He prescribed some spiritual passages, like Psalm 23, and told me to shed their light upon the shadows of fear in my mind. As he promised to hold me in his prayers, I remembered a children's book my grandparents had read to me, *The House with the Colored Window*. While the pony inside was really white, the different shades of tinted glass through which one peered into the house made it look green or red. By lifting the errors and doubts that filtered my view, I, like the character in the tale, would be able to see the purity within.

His contact with different Christian Science practitioners continued for almost three years. At the age of twenty Stephen left New York behind. His young adult years were an odyssey that led him first to Boston and then to Los Angeles. A skilled musician, he began to search for life and creativity in the study of composition and the rhythms of different ethnic groups. Wanting to travel the world and find spirit in the melodies of its cultures and peoples, Stephen took a job in the home improvement industry to earn what he needed to fund his trip. Unfortunately the bottom fell out of the Los Angeles housing market just after he arrived. With few resources and prospects, he took to living in his car and working at a plant nursery.

> I was a horrid gardener, hated the work, and I didn't know why I was in L.A. When my boss finally let me go, he said with real caring, "Steve, this is not what you're going to be." Knowing I needed work, a friend directed me to a health-food restaurant and market, Follow Your Heart. "Stephen," he assured me, "not only do they need somebody in produce, but this is your kind of place." Sure enough, everyone there was on some kind of spiritual search. Each of their paths seemed somewhat interesting and my coworkers invited me to observe their groups and gurus. I began to read and for the first time in a while started to again think about God.

To Dwell and to Seek

Stephen's early life story embodies many of the dynamics current in American culture and spirituality. Rather than residing in one locale, he moved from Detroit to Great Neck to Boston to Los Angeles. Rather than remaining with the doctrine and observances of a single denomination, his eclectic search led from Judaism to a sampling of various spiritual texts, Christian Science, Nichiren Buddhism, and ethnomusicology. Rather than trying to live a consistently good life by subscribing to the tenets and daily practices of one faith, Stephen's was a shifting search for spiritual experiences to answer questions and allay his fears.

Although Stephen derived a breadth and richness of insight from his far-ranging search, he also experienced loneliness and dissatisfaction. His words were poignant as he compared himself to his friends at Follow Your Heart: "Every one of them had a guru, a group, something they could hold on to. I felt like I was an outsider looking in."

I doubt that Stephen would undo any of his early spiritual adventures. But his confession indicates that they came at a price, the price of feeling grounded, of having resources and people you can depend on.

The Book of Psalms contains the following prayer: "One thing do I ask of the Lord, this do I seek. To dwell in the Lord's house all the days of my life. To gaze upon the splendor of the Lord and to visit within God's sanctuary." (Psalm 27:4) Although these words were written millennia ago, they articulate the burning need and spiritual paradox of our times. Is there a way to combine the freshness of discovery that visitors feel with the sense of continuity and belonging that residents come to know? In our desire to personally experience God's splendor can we seek and dwell at the same time?

Perhaps there is a way: a way to feel grounded and to search simultaneously, a way to hold onto both poles and to live in the creative tension of the two. A way to honor traditions and their ongoing practice while sensing God's unique movement within our own souls. A way open to long-time believers and to those who have had little or no religious training at all. A way that at one time was a feature of Roman Catholicism and Orthodox Christianity alone but is now gaining wider acceptance in Protestantism and non-Christian faiths. There is a way—the path of spiritual direction.

———————————

———————————————

Part Two

THE QUEST
FOR GUIDANCE

3

WHAT IS SPIRITUAL DIRECTION?

For myself and many others spiritual direction might best be described as a process that helps us recognize God's guidance that is there for us if only we are open to it.[1] It is a relationship between guide and seeker through which the guide helps the seeker detect God's movement within and to appreciate the divine plan that might underlie even the seemingly coincidental occurrences in life. It is about asking questions like:

- Where was God in your longing? Your success? Your pain?
- Where are you being led in your relationships? In your work?
- What are the implications of these insights for your daily life?
- What is illusion and what is truth?

Spiritual direction is a dynamic through which the guide helps the seeker listen for God's voice, not only through prayer and sacred texts, but through events and feelings, physical objects, and interactions with other people.

An Ancient Practice

Allusions to spiritual guidance can be traced back to antiquity. The Proverbs declare, "Many are the thoughts of the human heart, but God's guidance endures."[2] A more striking example of this adage can not be found than in the interactions between Moses and his father-in-law Jethro. Even later Islamic sources cite their relationship as a prime illustration of the need for spiritual direction.[3]

Exodus 18 describes a meeting that took place between Moses and Jethro following Israel's liberation from Egypt and the crossing of the Reed Sea. Having heard of the wonders God had performed, Jethro journeyed from Midian to reunite Moses with his wife, Zipporah, and their two sons. After a night of sacrifice and feasting, Jethro observed his son-in-law during the next day. Not only did Moses take no time for his family whom he hadn't seen in months, but he also spent every waking hour personally resolving each dispute in the camp.

Jethro, himself an experienced spiritual and political leader, recognized the danger in his son-in-law's arrogation of all responsibility and authority. He cautioned Moses against exhaustion and warned him that if he continued he would "debase himself and his people." He advised Moses to diffuse authority and empower more of God's people by appointing captains of tens, fifties, and hundreds, with Moses judging only the most demanding cases himself. Jethro then departed while Moses led the Israelites to the foot of Mount Sinai.

As a spiritual guide, Jethro displayed amazing insight. By watching Moses for one day he recognized his son-in-law's most glaring spiritual flaw: the placement of all religious authority with himself. Earlier, when the people complained for lack of water, Moses replied, "Why do you argue with me? Why do you test God?"[4] as if the former necessarily entailed the latter. Sadly, Jethro's warnings of debasement proved prophetic.

When Moses was delayed on Mount Sinai the people persuaded Aaron to make them a Golden Calf. Why? Not to replace God, but to replace Moses. To be a physical embodiment of the divine because, "this man Moses, who brought us out of the land of Egypt, we know not what has happened to him."[5] No one had the authority or even the will to stand against the idolaters. Later, after the first Tablets of the Covenant had been shattered, the idolaters purged, and new tablets carved, God reaffirmed the command for Israel to build the Tabernacle, a portable shrine. All Israel was to be involved in the donations and the construction, save one—Moses, who was not to participate until the very end. Would that Moses had heeded the observations of his spiritual guide, Jethro.

In his book *Spiritual Friend,* the Reverend Dr. Tilden Edwards also points to the contributions made by Greek and Roman thinkers to the development of spiritual direction. The term "Socratic method" is usually associated with pedagogic technique. The instruction begins by the mentor making an inquiry of the student. Then the give-and-take builds upon itself, leading the student to draw the desired conclusion for himself. However, Socrates' art of deep questioning prodded the disciple toward "a reverent, searching sense of life and of one's true place in it . . . abandoning the security of the unexamined life."[6] While this method of inquiry can, at times, leave the seeker unsure and confused, it radically challenges pat assumptions and opens one to see truth with unblinded eyes.

Pythagoras and the Stoic philosopher Seneca both suggested that we close our day by taking stock of our deeds, focusing on those that contribute to moral goodness. Seneca also pointed out the need for special counselors or "monitors" who would specify to their advisees those precepts needed to counteract the temptations of this world.

Cicero's dialogue *On Friendship* had an impact on the development of spiritual companioning. Unlike erotic love, this love of friends was not based on physical attraction or hope of gain. Instead it was expected to spring from caring, good will, and loyalty, so that each friend would take disinterested joy in the others' good fortune. Such friendship was later discouraged in Christian monasticism for fear it could lead to group fragmentation or lust. However, it did establish a model for two friends acting as spiritual companions, alternately offering support, advice, and critique, telling each other the truth in love.[7]

THE DESERT FATHERS AND LATER CHRISTIAN TRADITIONS

From its first chapters, the Bible seems to contrast the defiling effects of cities with the pristine reality of the desert. Cain, elder son of Adam and Eve and the world's first murderer, is also credited with being the first to establish a city.[8] Pithom and Ramses, the great Egyptian store cities, were built by Hebrew slave labor, and the urban culture of Egypt is decried with terms like "flesh pot" and is portrayed as being morally degenerate.[9] Conversely, the desert was viewed as a place where sin could be purged, moral character forged, and the surprising, miraculous care of God directly experienced.

> And you shall remember all the way which the Lord your God led you these forty years in the wilderness, to humble you and test you, to know what is your heart, if you would keep God's commandments or not. God humbled you, allowed you to hunger and fed you manna, which neither you nor your ancestors knew, to teach you that humans do not live by bread alone, but by all that issues from the mouth of the Lord do humans live.[10]

The Ten Commandments were given not in settled territory, but in the Sinai; and according to the prophets the desert was where Israel could prove its love for God. Thus Jeremiah declared, "So says the Lord: I remember the kindness of your youth, the love of your betrothal when you followed after me in the wilderness, in an unsown land."[11]

During the late Second Temple period, the Judean sect of the Essenes, who are credited with having written the Dead Sea Scrolls, left what they perceived to be the distortions of Jerusalem and its priesthood for a purer, more ascetic desert life. In the desert they could ready themselves to be the vanguard of the coming redemption. Essenes living outside Qumran who subscribed to this view probably influenced John the Baptist and Jesus and, through them, Saint Paul.

The Christian monastic movement, from which spiritual direction was born, drew upon these models.

From the end of the third through the beginning of the fifth century CE, thousands of Christians left behind Roman culture and its formalized, established Christian church. They lived alone or in ascetic groups in the deserts of Egypt, Syria, and Judea. The movement of spirit that motivated these people was typified by the experience of Abba (father) Arsenius in the fourth century:

> While still living in the palace, Abba Arsenius prayed to God in these words, "Lord, lead me in the way of salvation." And a voice came saying to him, "Arsenius, flee from men and you will be saved." Having withdrawn to the solitary life he made the same prayer again and he heard a voice saying to him, "Arsenius, flee, be silent, pray always, for these are the sources of sinlessness."[12]

To achieve salvation, those moved by the divine call—heard either as an inner voice or as mediated by scripture—would seek God through continual prayer and the silence of desert solitude. A third aspect of their spiritual program was the word of the Abba, the guidance that a spiritual father would give to younger monks. These words were not in the form of ongoing dialogue or debate. They were usually responses to individual questions and were viewed as sacraments to free the disciple to be led by the spirit of God.

At times the guidance might come as direct advice, as in this charge by the fourth-century saint, Abba Antony of Egypt: "Always have God before your eyes; whatever you do, do it according to the Holy Scriptures; in whatever place you live, do not leave it easily. Keep these three precepts and you will be saved."[13] The word also might be conveyed through a parable, an object lesson, or an act.

The relationship of the disciple to the spiritual father was one of obedience and permanence. However, the Abba's ultimate aim was to become superfluous to his spiritual child. His word and example would open the disciple to receive God's Holy Spirit, the true Guide of both their lives. Not viewing salvation as the exclusive domain of monks, the Desert Fathers made their counsel available to all who sought their guidance. Their belief was that "God is for all who choose Him, life for all, salvation for all . . . even as the outpouring of the light and the sight of the sun and the winds of heaven. . . ."[14]

The word that the Desert Fathers and their successors offered was geared specifically toward the spiritual development of the individual who came for guidance. Theirs was the task to discern the movement of spirits within the seeker, to help seekers identify those inclinations that would lead toward light, peace, charity, and humility, as well as those that would block the way to God, like the deadly sins of anger, pride, vainglory, envy, avarice, gluttony, lust, and sloth. The seeds of spiritual guidance first sown by the Desert Fathers continued to develop within Christianity throughout the centuries. The tradition of the solitary charismatic offering counsel and intercessory prayer continued in the Orthodox Church into this century in the figure of the sacred hermit, the Russian *poustinik*.[15]

The art of individual spiritual direction owes much to the writings of great sixteenth-century figures like Teresa of Ávila and John of the Cross. But perhaps the greatest Catholic contribution to the art of spiritual direction came from the writings of Ignatius Loyola, who emphasized not only the importance of attitude in disclosing the movement of spirits but also the importance of action.

Combining insight into the seeker's nature with knowledge of the Bible and the experience of his or her own spiritual journey, the Ignatian guide would aid the seeker in examining his or her life. What special knowledge could the seeker gain by reflecting on those instances when she felt desolate and in turmoil and on those moments that led to feelings of hope and consolation? Did the seeker feel that a gentle, small voice within or a pattern of external events was an invitation by God to pursue a certain path? Would that path, even if difficult, lead to a positive, joyful inner response and a good outer result? Or, would what initially appeared open and creative prove in the end to be self-serving, troubling, destructive, and even immoral? In addition to prayer, Ignatius suggested that seekers consider what decision they might make if faced with the moment of their own death or what decision an unknown person practicing perfection might make when choosing between paths.[16]

While the tradition of individual spiritual guidance remained strong in the Roman Catholic and Eastern Orthodox Churches, it was much less prevalent within Protestantism. Given the Protestant emphasis of the priesthood of all believers, guidance in that tradition was most often sought in personal prayer, reading the Bible, and involvement in a community of faith. Today, however, interest does seem to be growing among Protestants as well for ongoing individual and small group direction.[17]

WHAT MAKES SPIRITUAL DIRECTION UNIQUE?

For those seeking advice and counsel there are literally scores of options available in this therapeutic age. From radio talk shows to weekend retreats to self-help books, possibilities to enhance our growth beckon from all sides. Therefore, it might be worthwhile to distinguish the dynamics and objectives of spiritual guidance from other alternatives in general society and in the religious world. For our purposes let us examine the differences between spiritual guidance and psychotherapy on the one hand, and between spiritual guidance and pastoral counseling on the other.

The goal of psychotherapy is to help the patient gain a stronger sense of self, to adjust to the ups and downs of regular living.

> Most people see counselors or therapists because they are unhappy about not being "normal." They have difficulty relating to others or feel bad about themselves or have self-defeating habits that cause great suffering. They want to be like normal people, who presumably relate to others easily, feel good about themselves, and don't sabotage their own lives. Normal life certainly has its ups and downs, but psychological counseling and therapy can sometimes (but far from always) help people live better, normal, ordinary lives.[18]

Faced with unresolved issues from childhood, patients seek assistance from academically trained, certified therapists who help them explore their obsessions, compulsions, and fears. Among the techniques that the therapist may employ to help the patient resolve underlying psychological conflicts is transference. The patient might project wounded feelings from earlier relationships onto the therapist to work them through in a non-threatening, healing environment. The objective is for the therapist to help the patient resolve problems, at least in the short term, and to achieve a more healthy integration into society.

Pastoral counseling shares many features with psychotherapy. Just as the therapist is trained and certified, so, too, the pastoral counselor is academically prepared as an ordained clergyperson with special background in counseling and psychology. Both therapy and pastoral counseling help people adjust to the challenges in their lives and both focus on resolving problems, particularly in the short run. Both address questions of relationships and both, at times, can use transference.

Major differences between therapy and pastoral counseling can be found in two areas. While talk about God and spiritual experiences are taken quite seriously in pastoral counseling, some schools of psychology dismiss them as fanciful, if not delusional. Also, most therapists take an open-ended approach, helping patients draw conclusions and map courses of action that the patients feel are most authentic to themselves. While pastoral counselors are also concerned about the personal authenticity of those seeking advice, their guidance is usually conditioned by their world-view and beliefs and by the precepts of their denomination.

Unlike psychotherapy or even pastoral counseling, the focus of spiritual guidance is not on fortifying the self but on the unfolding relationship between that self and God. Rather than helping those seeking counsel adjust to everyday life, spiritual guidance points the seeker beyond the scope of the "normal," to see the self in relation to the divine that underlies and transcends the everyday. Although the spiritual guide might be an ordained clergyperson or may have completed a training program in spiritual direction, the main qualification is that the guide be receptive and "see to his own interior life and take time for prayer and meditation, since you never will be able to give others that which you don't have."[19] Since it is the guide's role to help nurture intimacy between the seeker and God, any transference of the seeker's feelings upon the guide (or worse, counter-transference of the guide's unresolved feelings upon the seeker) would be detrimental, shifting the focus away from God, the ultimate Guide of our lives.

While guide and seeker may well discuss the seeker's current and former relationships, these discussions are used to help see how those interactions relate to the seeker's primary relationship to God. A recounting of painful experiences might prompt the guide to ask questions like, "Where was God when this was unfolding?" or "Where do you think God is leading you?" After reflection, the seeker might begin to see that God could have been present in a teacher or friend who reached out to him or her during pain, or in the fortitude the seeker gained to go on. Or they may use that low as a springboard to further growth or greater empathy.

The guide might also help the seeker reconsider his or her view of God in light of these events, moving away from the concept of a punishing deity to the experience of a consoling presence who helps us draw straight with the crooked lines of our lives.

The experience of Susan Picotte, as reported by Cathy Grossman in *USA Today*, exemplifies the differences between spiritual guidance and the approaches of therapy and pastoral counseling. A nurse living in Goddard, Kansas, Susan was divorced from both her husband and from his Methodist Church. She no longer felt a connection to the Presbyterianism of her childhood and remained uninspired by the spiritual books she was reading. Rather than looking for psychological insights or reli-

gious counsel to help her adjust to her situation, Susan
sensed a different need. "My spiritual life was at a cross-
roads. I felt really lost and I wanted a guide for my journey." Instead of consulting a certified therapist or an
ordained member of the clergy, Susan sought guidance
from Phillip Saint Romain of the Heartland Center in
Great Bend, Kansas. Saint Romain is a Catholic layper-
son who is experienced as a Twelve-Step counselor and
who trained at the ecumenical Graduate Theological
Foundation in Donaldson, Indiana. Describing his work
with Susan and others as "spiritual companioning," he
claims that "finding faith, authenticity in love, and discernment of God in our lives is better done with others."
Guided by no psychological or denominational agenda,
he "helps people tune in their spiritual radio." "We can
talk about their marriage or their work or their kids," he
says, "But we always bring the conversation back to
God. How can we lighten their spiritual burdens or
enlighten their way.[20]

The lines separating spiritual guidance from other
forms of religious and nonreligious counsel are not set
and fast. Like a religious educator, a spiritual guide might
also teach a seeker a previously unknown biblical passage
or practice. Pastoral counselors can certainly be concerned about the client's relationship to God, and the
insights gained from spiritual direction can help seekers
move their problems toward resolution. Many of today's
therapists are quite sympathetic to the role that religious
faith plays in the lives of their patients and transpersonal
psychology sees mystical experience as something to be
sought. However, if we are looking to distinguish among
these approaches, the following breakdown might be
helpful:

- If you are interested in learning about the beliefs, observances, and texts of a religion because you want to know more or seek to more fully identify with that faith community, you are seeking *religious education or formation*.
- If you want to relieve your anxieties and learn how to understand and deal with their causes, you are seeking *psychotherapy*.
- If you want insight into how the wisdom of religious tradition might help you understand and respond to your problems, you are seeking *pastoral counseling*.
- If you wish to deepen your relationship with God so that you can recognize how God's spirit might be calling you and moving in your life, you are seeking *spiritual guidance*.

WHERE AM I?

What personal circumstances might lead a woman or man to seek spiritual direction? Let's consider the following tale. Rebecca was a wonderful young woman. She succeeded at work. She was liked by friends, neighbors, and just about everyone she met. She had a good heart and a giving soul. Rebecca also had a problem.

An early riser, Rebecca would awaken at the crack of dawn hoping to get a jump on her day. A single obstacle, however, continually held her back. You see—Rebecca simply could not find her clothes in the morning. Each day she'd tear through her closet and rummage through her drawers in search of that one certain outfit and its accessories. Blouses and skirts would fly through the air as Rebecca dashed around looking for that right combination she just knew was there, but that always evaded her reach.

One night Rebecca set upon a plan. Instead of facing another morning of frustration, she made a checklist of her next day's outfit and of the location of each garment. With her inventory complete, Rebecca went off to bed feeling more secure than she had in years.

Hours later the sun rose and so did Rebecca. She showered, groomed herself, and calmly picked up the list:

- Undergarments: top bureau drawer
- Stockings: second drawer down
- Blue dress: closet, fifth hanger from the left
- Shoes: underneath the bed
- Hat and coat: on the rack by the stairs

Confidently Rebecca located her clothes, donned them, and walked to the door. Ready to begin her daily journey, she made one final check of her things. Her smile slowly began to fade. Her head turned from side to side. Frantically she looked all about. Tears welled up in her eyes as she sank into a chair.

"I know where my dress, my shoes, and my stockings were. I know where my hat and coat and my bag are. But, now that I'm all ready to go, something is still missing. Where, oh where, in the name of God, am I?"

Many who seek spiritual direction come with Rebecca's question haunting them. Some feel that they have their daily routine down pat, with all their material belongings set exactly where they want them. Others may have been involved in a spiritual practice for years. They may have sampled various traditions, like Sarah and Stephen had. Or they may have thought that their own denomination, community, or beliefs held the key to overcoming chaos and setting life straight. Then, a transforming event, an unsettling doubt, or an upcoming challenge caused them to stop and reflect. Previously held religious prescriptions or secularist assumptions no longer seemed to suffice. The hunger for a personal connection to the Divine could not be satisfied by group imperatives alone. The need to recognize the spirit's movement within them, to locate their position and God's direction for them in this journey called life gave voice to Rebecca's plea, "Where, in the name of God, am I?"

Catherine Quinn is a member of the Society of the Holy Child of Jesus and an experienced spiritual director of more than thirty years. She observes that a variety of factors can lead a person to seek spiritual direction, to ask, "Where in God's name am I?" Some seekers wish to deepen their relationship with God and may want some help with their observance and prayer. Others might be facing a life decision or feel they are called to do something more for the world and aren't sure what that is. Finally there are those who come in the midst of, or shortly after, a time of crisis.[21]

Deborah Ann, an attorney who lives outside Washington, D.C., is a seeker from crisis.

> About three years ago, my spiritual life reached a significant turning point. Up until then, if someone asked me if I believed in God, I would have said yes, but without much conviction or understanding. . . . Then my mother died of a massive stroke. While my family was sitting in the hospital waiting room trying to decide whether to take my mother off life support, my father announces he has cancer. He doesn't tell us, but we learn from his doctor (the same day we removed my mother from life support) that it is terminal. Suddenly, I am my father's caregiver. Three

months later, he is dead. Five days before he died, my
father-in-law had a massive heart attack. I went from
caring for my father to supporting my husband and
in-laws in what turned out to be a fourteen-month
ordeal leading to my father-in-law's death. This was
the hardest, and yet the best (most meaningful, and
in some ways, most joyous) time of my life.

In this whole series of events, I found God. I
found God in accepting the connections I had with
these people with a whole heart, not as a burden, but
as a rich, painful, demanding, and ultimately joyous
blessing. I found God in the forgiveness and reconciliation that occurred between my father and me. I
found God in the community that rose around my
family and me and supported us. I never thought
myself capable of feeling or doing the things I did.
But as the prayer says, God answers before we call. I
never even had to fish out a quarter.

After my father died, I started to read many
books about spirituality, mostly Buddhist. I started
to meditate. After a year of doing this on my own,
and after my father-in-law died, so that now I had
the time and energy to devote to other things, I
wanted to explore this whole, new, rich unfolding
understanding with other people. I didn't seek spiritual direction (or didn't know that was what I was
looking for). I just thought I was looking for a class
or something that would help me to go deeper in my
still-new openness to God. Someone handed me a
brochure from Shalem, an interdenominational contemplative Christian center (why she thought I'd be
interested, I'll never know; we had never discussed
spiritual matters before then). I went to an open
house to see what Shalem was all about. I thought I
might take a body prayer class. Someone said something about a spiritual direction group starting in the
daytime, Tuesday mornings, one of my days off. I
wouldn't even have to take time away from my family (always an issue). I had no idea what spiritual
direction was, but those proverbial bells went off

for me. This seemed to offer what I was looking for, an opportunity to explore this whole new way of seeing the world and my relationship to it—to be with God—without having to make it "be" anything.

BETWEEN SEEKER AND GUIDE

What transpires within spiritual direction? Usually the seeker and guide will meet monthly for about an hour. The discussion can be far ranging, encompassing matters of devotional practice, the seeker's health, personal relationships, and challenges at work. However, according to Father George Aschenbrenner, head of the Jesuit Center for Spiritual Growth in Wernersville, Pennsylvania, the ultimate aim of the interaction is always to help the seeker gain closer union with God.[22]

That closer union often is effected through the medium of a tradition's scripture. If a seeker is feeling abandoned, a guide in the Jewish or Christian tradition might point to the promise of verses such as Genesis 49:3, ". . . you are my firstborn child. . . ." or Hosea 2:21, "I will betroth you unto me forever. . . ." Faced with life's turmoil the seeker may be asked to meditate daily on passages from the psalms such as, "Indeed for God let my soul be still, for from it comes my salvation" (Psalm 62:1), or "To You, Lord, silence is praise" (Psalm 65:1). Over the course of time the seeker may sense new perspectives or feelings of serenity arise. To show that God's care may be coming to the seeker from sources previously overlooked or even shunned, the seeker might be asked to read a selection like 2 Kings 7. That tale describes how four lepers became God's vehicles to lift Syria's siege of Israel's capital, Samaria, bringing salvation and sustenance to the starving people within its walls. The seeker might then reflect on those who reached out at a difficult moment or whose mere presence led to a sense of God's care. Just such a reflection is expressed in this anonymous vignette:

> Some months earlier my family and I had relocated from a different region of the country. In our former home we had hosted large holiday dinners with twenty or more people at our table. Those with whom we shared the joy of the season enlarged the spirit of celebration and community we had experienced.
>
> It seemed as if the first holiday spent in our new home was going to be quite different. Not only did we receive no invitations, but everyone we tried to invite had previous, long-standing engagements with their own families and friends. The prospect or our immediate family eating alone on the holiday reinforced our sense that we just didn't belong.
>
> When the holiday arrived I went off to services, feeling very much the outsider. After our prayers had finished I looked around the room. There was an elderly gentleman I barely knew. He was somewhat disheveled, in need of a shave, and not wearing any socks. When I asked him where he was going that night, tears welled up in his eyes. He began to speak of the family meals he had shared with his late wife and how her family would occasionally invite him for a holiday dinner. He cried as he told me that tonight was not one of those occasions, that he would return to his empty apartment and open a can of soup. Without hesitation I invited him to our home.
>
> Between the two of us I'm not sure who was the more grateful. On the way to our house a continuous loop played in my mind, "Thank you God for sending us a guest, thank you God for sending us a guest." From that time on our holidays were not complete without our new friend. Now that he is gone, our festive table always seems a little empty no matter how many others might be there.

The use of a journal can be valuable to spiritual reflection. Jotting down reactions to the events of the day, new insights gained through prayer, or the frustrations that come when one's aspirations or relationships to God and others seem blocked can reveal patterns unfolding over time. Sharing these observations with a guide helps uncover God's working in ways that might have gone undetected. One seeker relates the following:

> After years of being a successful therapist, burnout had taken its toll. I didn't want to get up in the morning, I barely got through my day, and I could only lay around and read at night. For months I was a black cloud whose presence in the house brought sorrow to my family.
>
> When my husband told me he was about to leave, I had no choice but to take action. I learned of an upcoming retreat, enrolled, and went off to the mountains for a week. It was there that I learned about spiritual direction and realized that perhaps this was one thing that had been missing from my life. When I returned home a priest was able to help me find a caring, responsive guide.
>
> Five years had passed, and, despite my best efforts, my marriage was again on the rocks. In a moment of despair I cried to my director asking why God was testing me so, questioning whether it was worth going on. My director, after consoling me, asked me to review my journal and to come back in two weeks. He promised to hold me in his prayers. When we examined the course of the past years some very interesting things came to light. Where once I had been impatient with some clients, my sense of compassion and understanding seemed to be growing. The recognition that I had always craved from my peers was taking a back seat to the importance of time spent with my family. Based on the insights gained from my own hurts, I had developed

some new approaches to counseling, which I introduced in my practice and shared at association meetings and in writing.

"What has God been telling you?" my director
asked.

"When I look back it seems that already, two
years ago, I began hearing the words, 'I the Lord, am
your healer.' Right after my husband told me he
thought our marriage was through, a verse from the
Psalms took hold of me, 'O Lord, I am your servant
born of your handmaid, you have loosed my bonds.'"

"Whether you realize it or not, it appears that
God had been leading you to greater freedom these
last years. And despite your pain—or, in more ways,
through it—God has been offering you untold grace."

Dumbstruck, I could only nod my head. It
seemed like forever that I sat in prayerful silence,
amazed and filled with thanks.

As implied above, prayer, in its many forms, lies at
the heart of spiritual guidance. The director might suggest that seekers regularly recite prayer verses appropriate to them throughout the day. These could include, for
Jews or Christians respectively, "I set the Lord before me
always" (Psalm 16:8), or the Lord's Prayer, (Our Father
Who art in heaven . . .), or a form of the Jesus prayer (Lord
Jesus Christ, Son of God, have mercy upon me, a sinner.
Seekers of other traditions may be asked to select a liturgical scriptural verse and repeat its words slowly over and
over while remaining still for an initial period of five to ten
minutes daily. Over the course of time these practices can
allow God's voice to break into the seeker's consciousness
through the clutter of noise and the ego structure that
usually dominates our lives.

Another proposal might be for the seeker to worship more regularly as part of a congregation. Inspiration

can come from feeling addressed by the words of the sermon or by chanting hymns and sharing in rituals and sacraments, in joys and sorrows, with others in the community. A sense of personal sanctity can flow from harmonizing one's own schedule with the rhythm of the liturgical calendar year.

Prayer is also an essential aspect of the relationship between seeker and guide. After a first meeting both might pray individually, asking God's insight as to the appropriateness of establishing this guidance relationship. As each session begins the seeker may ask God to lend an ear and support them while praying in words like: "God, give us your perspective on what has been happening. How have you been present? How have you been addressing me through my thoughts, my feelings, my work, my relationships? What have you been trying to teach me about you? About me? What is your prayer for me now? What do you want from me?"[23]

Between sessions the guide will carry the seeker in his or her own prayers, asking for God's care on the seeker's behalf. The presence or absence of the guide's own willingness to pray for the seeker can be an important sign as to whether this guidance relationship is a proper match.

THE BENEFITS OF SPIRITUAL DIRECTION

Genesis 21 records a fascinating tale about Ishmael and his mother Hagar. Having to leave Abraham's tents as the result of a family feud, mother and son embarked upon a desert journey. Soon the teenage Ishmael was consumed by sunstroke, and as the water ran out Hagar didn't know what to do. Unable to bear the agony of seeing her son die, she placed him under the shade of a bush and went

off a distance and began to cry. Suddenly an angel called
to Hagar, and in the midst of her tears she gained assur-
ance that God had heard her cry and Ishmael's voice. She
was called to arise, to lift Ishmael and "strengthen her
hand through his." God then opened her eyes and she
beheld a well containing water to quench her thirst and
that of her ailing son. With renewed strength and a sense
of mission, Hagar and Ishmael resumed their journey to
Paran. Ishmael became an archer, married an Egyptian
woman, and went on to be the father of a great nation.

Although most guides today are of the earthly variety, in a real sense the angel acted as Hagar's spiritual
director. The Hebrew term for an angel, *malach,* literally
means a "messenger" (as does the Greek *angelos*). In the
midst of this difficult situation, it was the angel who
helped Hagar discern God's unfolding message in her life.
Hagar was in despair. She lost her home, and she faced
losing her son as well. When the angel called to her,
"What is it Hagar?" the Old Testament records no
response. Perhaps in the midst of her tears she was
unable to speak. The angel then offered words of reassurance, "Don't fear." Why? Not because there was no
danger, but because she and Ishmael had not been abandoned. God was with them in the moment, as they were:
God "has heard the voice of the boy *from where he is.*"
Hagar was then called to perform a caring act, to lift
Ishmael. She learned that through this act she would be
empowered, that she would "strengthen her hand
through his."

After the angel's visit, God opened Hagar's eyes,
and she saw a well. The Bible does not indicate that God
then made the well appear miraculously. The movement
of God's salvation was more subtle, lifting the blinders of

desolation so that Hagar could see what had always been there and could draw from it life sustaining waters. Refreshed by the waters and by a new realization of purpose, Hagar and Ishmael took up their journey once again.

Unlike Hagar, most of us need more than one meeting with our spiritual guide. However, the blessings and the challenges that Hagar experienced continue to be quite real. What are they? A sense of reassurance, of personally being called and heard and accepted by God. The realization that God is with us when we walk and when we fall. The summons to have God act through us as we help others and the knowledge that we gain strength from these acts. The ability to see with newly opened eyes the potential for divine healing in resources previously overlooked. The fortitude to rise and resume life's journey having been transformed.

In their book *Jewish Spiritual Guidance,* Carol Ochs and Kerry Olitzky describe both the personal transformation and the qualities of spirit and experience that can serve as signposts along the path of spiritual direction.[24]

Joan, one of their seekers, developed a model for perceiving the direction of God's movement through the significant changes in her life. Her schema, based on the work of Aristotle as filtered through the lens of twelfth-century Jewish philosophy, sets forth six different forms of motion:

- Coming to be—what has become real now that wasn't before?
- Passing away—what contentious aspects of our past experience will we leave behind?
- Increase—what traits do we see growing stronger?

- Decrease—what characteristics will wane?
- Locomotion—what external change in job, status, relationships, and locale are occurring and where might they be leading?
- Becoming other—what internal transformations have unfolded which provide us with a totally new perspective on living?

This model resonates with the experiences we saw earlier of the psychologist and the "holiday host." The psychologist had been preoccupied with status and professional recognition. Family and, at times, even the comfort of her patients took a back seat. Her hearing the verse from the psalms, ". . . you have loosed my bonds," foretold the passing away of one chapter of her life as a new one was coming into being. Her patience and understanding increased as her desire to seek status waned. And while a change in her marital status seemed imminent, her cherishing of family and ability to teach and heal from her own wounds indicated that she was becoming other than she had been. Similarly, the locomotion that moved the "holiday host" and his family to their new locale seemed to point him toward their first guest and to a deep appreciation of the blessings even unlikely others can bring just by being there.

This process is not one of continual progress. It has its fits and starts, its backtracking and advances. Yet along this road toward spiritual understanding you begin to experience special qualities within, qualities of wholeness, peace, and clarity of purpose. Like Hagar, you become able to face certain fears and feel empowered to move forward. You begin to show a new tenderness toward others and yourself, and feel a release of inner joy.[25]

Evidence of just such an unfolding of traits can be found in the following account:

> Last month when I was walking to work I saw a homeless person sleeping on the street. She was there every day, and every day I tried to avoid looking at her. Then I started to leave a bag of food for her. Finally one day I stopped and took a good look at her. I realized she had something to say to me about myself. I feel so restless and so homeless. I pray every day for about ten minutes with Scripture. One day I opened to the verse where Jesus said, "Make your home in me." I felt that He was talking directly to me.[26]

4

Looking Beyond Your Own Faith

My Journey

As we have seen, the blessings of spiritual direction are many. But why would someone seek guidance outside his or her own faith, particularly if they are well grounded in their own tradition? Perhaps my experiences can offer some insight.

In many ways my parents' home on Chicago's far South Side embodied the 1950s "spirituality of settlement." Although neither my mom nor my dad had received much in the way of formal Jewish training, they wanted to provide both of their sons with the religious foundation they had not had. Our existence literally revolved around the life of our Conservative synagogue, Rodfei Shalom-Or Hadash.[1] My mother's involvement began as gift shop chairwoman and continued through to her election as president of the sisterhood. My father served on the congregational board, coordinated the reserved sanctuary seating for the High Holy Days (no small task), and cochaired the Jewish Committee on Scouting. Hebrew school, choir, scouts, Torah reading club, youth activities, and services seemed to fill every waking hour my brother and I didn't spend at school or doing homework. Even sports were played in United Synagogue Youth and B'nai B'rith Leagues. Each Friday night, without fail, the Addisons lit Sabbath candles, recited our table prayers, and went together after dinner to late evening services.

Much of my adult life represented a continuation of the themes that had developed during my childhood. More than one friend asked me if I had left Chicago at eighteen to attend the University of Illinois or merely to spend most of my time at its Jewish Student Center, the Hillel Foundation. After earning my B.A., I went off to New York to study for ordination at the Jewish Theological Seminary, supporting myself by teaching Hebrew school and leading youth groups, as did most of my classmates. Graduation day arrived; we collected the title *rabbi* together with our diplomas and went off to teach, counsel, and minister to the Jewish community.

During those years I was privileged to study with world-class scholars whom I felt took a real interest in my development: Dr. Seymour Segel, Dr. Moshe Zucker, and the revered Dr. Abraham Joshua Heschel. Not only did I learn Bible and rabbinics, but I was also able to concentrate on my loves: Jewish philosophy and mysticism. Only one problem existed. Although today's curriculum and orientation are different, at that time the seminary's exclusively critical historical approach to study seemed to reduce all of Judaism to a left-brain exercise. We investigated the evolution and comparative meaning of concepts like *ruchaniyut* (spirituality) and *penimiyut* (inwardness). However, no one provided us with any counsel or introduced us to practices that might have helped transform these ideas into the inner realities of our spiritual lives.

I remember arriving at the seminary for my preliminary interviews. At the age of twenty I had been inspired by my studies of comparative religion at the University of Illinois. I was indebted to two young rabbis, my Hillel director, Edward Feld, and my philosophy professor at Chicago's Spertus College of Judaica, Byron Sherwin, for introducing me to the challenges and wisdom of Jewish thought. Sitting before the dean of admissions, I voiced my interest in exploring new forms of worship and liturgical expression that might inspire our deepest feelings. His response was crisp and direct. "That is all well and good, Mr. Addison. However, the Jewish Theological Seminary is an institution for the study of the classical texts."

Duly chastened, I took up the task of studying those texts, observing the Torah's ethical and ritual commandments known as *mitzvot,* and preparing myself so I could join my fellow students in the service of world Jewry. Our underlying credo seemed to embody the rabbinic prescription, *Lo hamidrash haikar elah hamaaseh,* "It is not exposition that is essential, only acts."

During the next eighteen years I threw myself into my rabbinate, first as a Hillel director then as a pulpit rabbi. In the midst of my denominational and communal busy-ness I was occasionally reminded that something might be amiss with my spiritual life. One year I reviewed my High Holy Day sermons with my then mother-in-law. I told her I was going to discuss the problems of Israel and world Jewry as well as some issues of social injustice facing us in Chicago. "Howard," she said, "that all sounds quite exciting, but aren't you going to speak to the inner person at all?" Dumbfounded, I literally didn't know how to respond.

Similarly, I was surprised by a comment written on a personal theology paper I had submitted to fulfill a doctoral requirement at the Chicago Theological Seminary. On the last page my professor had written, "This is the most secular essay I've ever read." True, it didn't speak of God's movement within my own life, but it was replete with references to biblical and rabbinic sources, as I had been taught to write at the Jewish Theological Seminary. So what was the problem?

There is a saying, "life intervenes," and by 1994 it surely had. In many ways the previous eleven years had not been kind. My first marriage ended in divorce. Four of my nearest and dearest lost their lives: one by suicide, one in a car crash, and two by cancer. My mother's failing health had rendered her a cardiac cripple requiring frequent hospitalizations.

Despite a routine of study and daily worship, I felt depleted and empty inside. Outwardly I played the role of a fairly successful congregational rabbi; in my heart of hearts I cynically felt like a huckster for God. Teaching, programming, conducting worship, and helping to develop institutions came easily. Counseling, visiting the sick, and consoling the bereaved were tasks I performed, sometimes well, but the need to be fully present in those moments always seemed beyond my comfort zone. Always giving at the office left me little to give at home.

With my life in shambles I called the Rabbinical Assembly and basically cried, "Help!" Elliot Schoenberg, our director of Rabbinic Services, suggested I call the

Alban Institute, an interdenominational Christian center near Washington, D.C., dedicated to the ongoing training and support of congregations and clergy. During the next eight months I attended two of their seminars. On a practical level I learned of the need to balance my personal, professional, and spiritual lives and to assess my priorities and talents in relation to my synagogue's expectations. Socially I found support and nurture from colleagues who were experiencing the same conflicts I was. But the most profound impact of these seminars was on my spiritual life.

Over the years I had maintained my interest in kabbalah, Jewish mysticism. I continued to read and teach classes on it at continuing education institutes and on the undergraduate level. My approach was that of my training—long on historical analysis, very short on practice—with no attention paid to how God might transform your inner life. At the Alban seminars we joined in chant and guided imagery, in prayer expressed through body movement and through meditation on God's gift of breath. We learned how our different personality types reveal our deepest motivations and help determine the different ways in which we pray. And, for the first time, I heard the term *spiritual direction*.

Like most clergy I was well acquainted with the dynamics of pastoral counseling, having been trained to offer such help to those in need. Spiritual direction seemed to be counsel of a very different sort. The opportunity to interact with a guide, not to solve practical problems, but to deepen my relationship with God, was what I had been lacking most. I longed to discern how God's spirit might be moving in my rabbinate and in my personal life, how as a descendent of Abraham I could fulfill God's charge, "walk before Me and be wholehearted."[2]

One obstacle, however, blocked my quest. Where, as a non-Orthodox Jew, could I find such guidance? Many *yeshivot* (talmudic academies) have *mashgichim* (religious supervisors) who direct the yeshivah students on matters of observance and religious character development. Hasidic communities are served by *mashpi'im* (prompters) among whose tasks it is to help newcomers adapt to the Hasidic way of life. However, in reaction to Orthodoxy's constraints on personal autonomy, the leaders of Conservative, Reform, and Reconstructionist Judaism historically had refrained from offering any counsel that might intrude on the freedom of one's religious inquiry. Prescribed observance within the parameters of denominational practice—somewhat; doing anything that might seem to prescribe one's thoughts or feelings—never.[3]

Not knowing where to turn within my own tradition, I called Father Richard Rohr, a Franciscan priest whose tapes on spirit and personality type had moved me during my Alban seminars. I phoned his Center for Action and Contemplation in New Mexico and told him that I was a rabbi in Fort Lauderdale seeking spiritual direction as a non-Christian, preferably with a guide acquainted with the Enneagram[4] system of personality typing. He asked how far I was from Lantana, Florida, and I told him not too far, about a fifty minute drive. He replied, "Some years ago I conducted a retreat at the Cenacle House in Lantana. There are some very wise women there. Why don't you look them up?"

Well, look them up I did, and since then I have been in direction with the Sisters of the Cenacle, a Catholic religious order dedicated to offering spiritual guidance. In a very real sense it is only since then that I have begun to recognize God's transforming presence in my life. Like

Hagar at the well I felt that my eyes were finally being opened to the unfolding wonder of intimacy with God, wonder that had always been present had I just known where and how to look.

INTERFAITH SPIRITUAL DIRECTION IN FORMER TIMES

Historical examples going back to antiquity reveal occasions when persons of one faith sought direction from guides of another. One such instance is recorded in the *Questions of King Menander*. Menander, a Greek monarch who ruled in northwest India during the middle of the second century BCE, engaged in a series of discussions with the Buddhist sage Nagasena. According to tradition, Menander was so moved by their relationship that he imprinted one of its symbols, the eight-spoked wheel, on the coins of his realm. The following account describes how Nagasena turned a public dispute into an occasion for Menander to reflect on the composite nature of the human soul:

> Then King Menander went up to the Venerable Nagasena, greeted him respectfully, and sat down. Nagasena replied to the greeting, and the King was pleased at heart. Then King Menander asked: "How is your reverence known, and what is your name?"
>
> "I'm known as Nagasena, your Majesty, that's what my fellow monks call me. But though my parents may have given me such a name . . . it's only a generally understood term, a practical designation. There is no question of a permanent individual implied in the use of the word."
>
> "Listen, you five hundred Greeks and eight thousand monks!" said King Menander. "This Nagasena has just declared that there's no permanent individuality implied in his name!" Then, turning to Nagasena,

"If, Reverend Nagasena, there is no permanent individuality, who gives you monks your robes and food,
lodging and medicines? And who makes use of
them? Who lives a life of righteousness, meditates,
and reaches Nirvana? Who destroys living beings,
steal, fornicates, tells lies, or drinks spirits? . . . If
what you say is true there's neither merit nor demer-
it, and no fruit or result of good or evil deeds. If
someone were to kill you there would be no question
of murder. And there would be no masters or teachers in the Buddhist Order and no ordinations. If your
fellow monks call you Nagasena, what then is
Nagasena? Would you say your hair is Nagasena?"

"No, your Majesty."

"Or your nails, teeth, skin, or other parts of your
body, or the outward form, or sensation, or perception, or the psychic constructions or consciousness?
Are any of these Nagasena?"

"No, your Majesty."

"Then for all my asking I find no Nagasena.
Nagasena is a mere sound! Surely what your
Reverence has said is false!"

Then the Venerable Nagasena addressed the King.

"Your Majesty, how did you come here—on foot,
or in a vehicle?"

"In a chariot."

"Then tell me what is the chariot? Is the pole the
chariot."

"No, your Reverence."

"Or the axle, wheels, frame, reins, yoke, spokes
or goad?"

"None of these things is the chariot."

"Then all of these separate parts taken together
are the chariot?"

"No, your Reverence."

"Then is the chariot something other than the
separate parts?"

"No, your Reverence."

"Then for all my asking, your Majesty, I can find
no chariot. The chariot is a mere sound. What then is

the chariot? Surely what your Majesty has said is false! There is no chariot! . . ."

When he had spoken the five hundred Greeks cried, "Well done!" and said to the King, "Now, your Majesty, get out of that dilemma if you can!"

"What I said is not false," replied the King. "It's on account of all these various components, the pole, axle, wheels, and so on, that the vehicle is called a chariot. It's just a generally understood term, a practical designation."

"Well said, your Majesty! You know what the word *chariot* means! And it's just the same for us all. It's on account of the various components of my being that I'm known by the generally understood term, the practical designation Nagasena."[5]

Illness and the desire for healing also provided historic opportunities for interfaith spiritual direction. Naaman, general of the Aramean army during the ninth century BCE, had been afflicted with leprosy. Unable to find a cure in Syria, Naaman learned of the existence of a Samarian prophet, Elisha, from his wife's maid, an Israelite captive. After an exchange of correspondence between the kings of Aram and Israel, Naaman embarked on a journey to meet the wonder worker.

So Naaman came with his horses and chariots and halted at the door of Elisha's house. Elisha sent a messenger to say to him, "Go and bathe seven times in the Jordan, and your flesh shall be restored and you shall be clean." But Naaman was angered and walked away. "I thought," he said, "he would surely come out to me, and would stand and invoke the Lord his God by name, and would wave his hand toward the spot, and cure the affected part. Are not the Amanah and the Pharpar, the rivers of Damascus, better that all the waters of Israel? I could bathe in them and be clean!" And he stalked off in a rage.

But his servants came forward and spoke to him. "Sir," they said, "if the prophet told you to do something difficult, would you not do it? How much more when he has only said to you, 'Bathe and be clean.'" So he went down and immersed himself in the Jordan seven times, as the man of God had bidden; and his flesh became like that of a little boy, and he was clean. Returning with his entire retinue to the man of God, he stood before him and exclaimed, "Now I know that there is no God in the whole world except in Israel! So please accept a gift from your servant." But Elisha replied, "As the Lord lives, whom I serve, I will not accept anything." Naaman pressed Elisha to accept, but he refused. And Naaman said, "Then at least let your servant be given two mule-loads of earth; for your servant will never again offer up burnt offering or sacrifice to any god, except the Lord. But may the Lord pardon your servant for this: When my master enters the temple of Rimmon to bow low in worship there, and he is leaning on my arm so that I must bow low in the temple of Rimmon, may the Lord pardon your servant in this." And Elisha said to him, "Go to peace."[6]

What began as a search for a physical cure was transformed into a powerful moment of spiritual guidance. Naaman learned that God's healing need not be accompanied by the waving of hands, the cry of "heal, heal!" or any other such theatrics. Having realized that his illness had brought him to experience the power of God, Naaman became a changed man from his skin to the depths of his soul. However, he had a practical problem: how to keep his military office, since it required worshipping the idol Rimmon together with his king. When Naaman alerted Elisha to his plight and the possible resolution of Naaman continuing public idol worship while building his own private altar to God, Elisha sent him away with the words, *Lech l'shalom* (Go to peace). This expression can mean "farewell" or can be used idiomatically in Hebrew to tell someone to go to his final peace— to "drop dead." Perhaps Elisha as spiritual guide used this ambiguous phrase purposely. He genuinely wished Naaman well but prompted him to consider whether pretending to worship Rimmon counter to his own beliefs might constitute a form of real inner death.

Finally there were times of cross-faith interactions when a seeker's request not only changed the seeker but provided an object lesson for others as well. Such was the case when a Canaanite woman asked Jesus to exorcise a demon that had possessed her daughter:

> Then Jesus went from that place and withdrew to the region of Tyre and Sidon. And behold, a Canaanite woman of that district came and called out, "Have pity on me, Lord, Son of David! My daughter is tormented by a demon." But he did not say a word in answer to her. His disciples came and asked him, "Send her away, for she keeps calling out after us." He said in reply, "I was sent only to the lost sheep of the house of Israel." But the woman came and did him homage, saying, "Lord, help me." He said in reply, "It is not right to take the food of the children and throw it to the dogs." She said, "Please, Lord, for even the dogs eat that which falls from the table of their masters." Then Jesus said to her in reply, "O woman, great is your faith! Let it be done for you as you wish." And her daughter was healed from that hour.[7]

Not only did the woman gain a cure for her daughter, but the New Testament portrays Jesus as using this woman's faith to demonstrate to those around him that his guidance and blessings are open to all.

MODERN MOTIVATIONS

Intellectual curiosity and the desire for physical or spiritual healing prompted Menander, Naaman, and the Canaanite woman to seek help from guides outside of their own traditions. What leads those who could be considered their spiritual descendants to do the same today?

Some, like myself, look beyond our own communities simply out of a question of availability. Generally we feel comfortable in our traditions and are dedicated to their beliefs and practices. However, guidance that focuses on deepening one's relationship with God might not be readily attainable within our communities. Or it might only be offered in a stream of our tradition not open to us. Or perhaps we just do not know where to look.

Others, while not wishing to convert, might feel positively attracted to a certain faith or to a particular guide from that faith. Bob, a third-generation Italian-American Catholic who himself offers spiritual guidance in Rochester, New York, described it this way: "In high school I became interested in Eastern traditions. Buddhism seemed to have the language to express the experience I was having."

Radha is a chemical engineer who lives in Oregon. She is a descendent of a prominent Hindu Brahmin, or priestly, family who for generations served as religious and political consultants to the rulers of the Mogul empire. Her family came to the United States during the 1970s, initially settling in Indianapolis, Indiana. When asked about her family's religious practice, Radha said:

> Like most Hindu families, the majority of our sacred observances were done at home. Attendance at the temple is usually reserved for special occasions, like

the offering of a baby's shorn hair to the gods three to five months after birth. This rite, which my own niece recently celebrated, marks the time when a family ritually claims their child from the province of the gods.

My parents' home has a special sacred room set aside near the kitchen. Inside are statues of Sri Venkatesvara and his wife. Sri Venkatesvara is revered as the embodiment of divine scholarship and is believed to be an *avatar*, or incarnation, of the god Vishnu. My family's devotion to Sri Venkatesvara stems from the fact that in past generations they were the interpreters of the *Vedas*, the Hindu scriptures, to the Muslim Mogul rulers.

To this day, my mother still participates weekly in the *pujah* ceremony. Each Saturday she meticulously cleanses herself, puts on specially cleaned clothing, cuts flowers and offers them to the gods.

While Radha views her move to America as beneficial, it was not without its costs. She and her sister were separated from the rest of the family, remaining in India for two and a half years until they were all reunited in America. As a young woman she tried to address her resulting insecurities through psychotherapy.

My therapy sessions did help some. The clinical approach was good at dealing with those fears and their underlying causes that we could pinpoint. However, it didn't address my soul. I was still left with a kind of nebulous emptiness. I needed to live with a sense of reverence, a sense of sanctity. Something was still missing.

Although her brother is a devotee of Sai Baba, Radha didn't feel that consulting a swami or a guru was right for her. Having grown up in the United States from the time she was eight, she admits that her cultural outlook is decidedly Western. A friend recommended that she consult

Dale Rhodes, a spiritual guide at the Interfaith Spiritual Center in Portland, Oregon. Although Dale identifies with the Unitarian Universalist Association and Radha remains a Hindu, she feels that theirs is a wonderful guidance match.

> Dale is the perfect sounding board. His mentoring integrates both the movement of the spirit and the needs of daily life. He reminds me that we all carry within us a spark of the Divine which needs to be honored at each moment.
>
> This teaching parallels our Hindu concept of *atman,* the inner soul, which is also viewed as being an aspect of Divinity. This similarity reaffirms my conviction that all faiths have a common sacred core. Dale and I might have different doctrinal religious beliefs, but our spiritual beliefs are the same. I really do have the best of both worlds.

Unlike Radha, Michael Green, an artist and writer, grew up without any formal religious background. He offered this account of how he came to seek guidance from the Sufi master, Bawa Muhaiyaddeen:

> As a child I grew up in West Nyack, New York, and was basically raised outside of religion. My parents were both liberal intellectuals—open-minded, but God was not particularly on the table. In one sense, that lack of religious upbringing was a blessing because it didn't leave me with any spiritual biases or resentments that needed to be undone in later life.
>
> My first inkling of a spiritual revelation came during the sixties. I was an undergraduate at New York University's uptown campus. One afternoon I was just lying on the grass, looking up at the trees adorning the park on Washington Square. Watching the sway of the leaves and branches, it overwhelmingly came to me that this world is composed not just of atoms and protons. The universal glue that holds

everything together is love. More than a mere abstraction, love is the field that bonds all of reality.

Soon after that a friend asked if I wanted to help out with a light show that Professor Timothy Leary, a pioneer in psychedelics, was presenting at a theater in Greenwich Village. That request began a personal odyssey that led me to Leary's community in Mill-brook, New York, out to California, and then back to the East Coast and Woodstock, New York.

If I had a tradition then, it was the tradition of the North American hippie movement. I really had no problem with any religion. Everything was fine! When I was at Millbrook someone gave me *The Gospel of Ramakrishna,* the Indian teacher who per-sonally experienced the universal core in all religious faiths. I literally devoured his teachings and began to see myself as some kind of home-grown *sadhu,* or wandering renunciant. I met various spiritual teach-ers but none of them clicked. More and more I felt like I had karmic "dirt on my neck." No matter which way I turned I couldn't quite see it to clean it off by myself.

Through some unusual quirks of fate I wound up acquiring twelve acres of land near Woodstock and was living in a tipi on top of a hill. One day while help-ing with a dome-raising for a free school, I met Jonathan Granoff (now an important international nuclear disarmament activist and interfaith advocate). Immediately we sensed that we were kindred souls. We agreed that the next step in our lives was to find a spiritual teacher who, having transcended the con-cerns and boundaries of the ego, had merged with the Ultimate. We agreed that if either of us ever met such a guide, someone, as we referred to it, "where nobody was home," we'd call the other right away. Sure enough, a few months later, Jonathan called.

"Michael, I've found the teacher in Philadelphia. He is a Sufi master and his name is Guru Bawa."

I hitchhiked down from the Catskills until I arrived at a nondescript row house in West Philadelphia. I entered and was struck by the energy of the small community present. Was this the same feeling of grace that had been present among the first Christians? Someone led me upstairs to Guru Bawa's room. Of course then, in the early seventies, the term *guru* hadn't yet been debased by the excesses of some other Eastern teachers, excesses which moved Bawa to drop that title which he felt was an honorific that had unfortunately become tainted. As I stood in a narrow corridor this slight man appeared at the far end, walked past and gave me a nod and a smile. Luminous eyes! There was this instant recognition that this was an encounter with some very non-ordinary reality. I often described him as "beamed in from the center of the universe."

It was the custom of Bawa and his followers to take a nap in the afternoon. So I laid down too in one of the living rooms on the lower level. As I slipped into a half-sleeping and half-awake state, I felt a living presence drop down from above and enter my chest. It was as if my heart was solid butter and here was a mold giving it shape and coherence. Although another year of probing and questions would pass before I fully accepted Bawa as my spiritual guide, or "father" as he preferred to be understood, it was at that moment that I first felt as if his seal had been stamped upon my being.

While some seekers are attracted to the teaching of their guide's faith or to the guide as a person, others consciously choose interfaith spiritual direction because they feel wounded or just wish to gain distance from their own traditions. As one seeker bluntly stated, "I wanted to follow my own agenda, not my religion's agenda for me." Similarly, a guide who offers direction for military personnel reported that three gay individuals have recently sought him out. Each claimed that they thought the guide's faith tradition would allow him to be more open to them than a guide from their own tradition would be.

Deborah Ann, the attorney from Chapter 3 who turned to spiritual direction after prolonged illness and death in her family, describes her lack of familiarity and discomfort with Judaism as a motivating factor for seeking guidance from beyond home.

> My relationship with Judaism very much paralleled my relationship with my parents: I loved them but I didn't know them very well. Something always seemed to be blocking my way; like being Jewish was a club and I didn't know the password. I had tried an adult bat mitzvah class and, through no fault of anyone, it confirmed my view that as a woman who hadn't gone to Sunday School, who didn't have children, and who couldn't make a perfect challah, there wasn't much of a place for me. I still wanted a connection with Judaism, but I didn't see any Jewish opportunities for talking about God. Ethics, right living, arguing disembodied points of Torah and Talmud, learning Hebrew, lessons on how to appropriately celebrate the holidays—but nothing where I could talk about what God meant to me, what God was doing to me. I thought a Jewish group or class would come down to "do you keep a kosher home?" That's not where I wanted to start with God.

SOCIETAL TRENDS

The statements above reflect deeply personal reasons for seeking interfaith spiritual direction. There, are however, some identifiable societal trends that might help us understand why people from certain faiths seem to move toward certain others.

In his *History of Christian Spirituality*,[8] Urban T. Holmes described four different types of spirituality. Drawing upon his work, Corinne Ware developed the Spirituality Wheel, a basic test with separate Jewish and

Christian versions that helps individuals recognize their
own spiritual preferences and those of their religious
institutions.[9]

The different categories of spirituality are placed in
four quadrants determined by the intersection of two
lines. The vertical line is bound by the terms *speculative,*
that which engages the mind, and *emotional,* that which
moves the heart. At either end of the horizontal line is the
Revealed God, as described by religious imagery, and
God the Mystery, defying and transcending all description. When brought together the diagram looks like this:

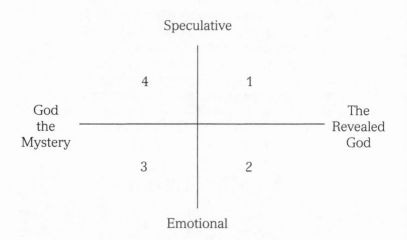

Type One spirituality draws upon thinking and the
revealed word. This form of religious expression is best
represented by the study of scripture, the set liturgy of the
service, and the sermon.

The spirituality of Type Two still invokes God through verbal images, but is emotional in nature. This expression stresses personal witnessing, rousing music, and a sense of being reborn.

Moving to the left side of the diagram, the spirituality of Type Three again appeals to our feelings, but here the emphasis is on hearing God, or mystical union, rather than speaking to or about God. This is the spirituality of meditation and mysticism, of chant and breath prayer, of visualization and silent retreat, of allowing the "still small voice" to break through.

Finally, Type Four is best expressed by the phrase "My life and works are my prayer." In Christianity this is the Social Gospel. No one better articulated this form of spirituality than Dr. Abraham Joshua Heschel when he described his march with the late Dr. Martin Luther King, Jr. in Selma, Alabama: "I felt as if my feet were praying."

This diagram is helpful in categorizing the varying forms of religious expression, and it leads to some important insights. It teaches that all four types, and not any one of them alone, qualify as spirituality, what Lawrence Kushner defines as "that dimension of living in which we are aware of God's presence."[10] The four quadrants can also help us understand the direction of movement between faiths.

One of the most insightful observations of the Spirituality Wheel is that an overemphasis of the spirituality in any given type can be balanced by the religious expression of its diagonal opposite. Those who stress the spiritual emotionalism of Type Two might become so concerned with their own group's salvation that they see others as damned. This group needs the balance of dedication to the godly serving of others found in Type Four.

Conversely, those who exclusively emphasize Type Four spiritual practice might become so engrossed in human social activism as to lose their personal connection to the Divine. They need an infusion of Type Two's religious zeal to reinstill a sense of God's presence in their lives.

Given this dynamic we now might better understand why so many Christians have moved from mainstream denominations to Evangelical churches and why a wildly disproportionate number of Jewish seekers have flocked to the spiritual inwardness of various Asian religions. Rodger Kamenetz's *The Jew in the Lotus*[11] highlights the number of Jewish-born seekers who have left Judaism in favor of Buddhism, and studies indicate that Roman Catholicism and mainstream Protestantism are shrinking while Evangelical churches grow.[12]

I have heard Episcopal and Congregationalist (United Church of Christ) clergy describe their denominations as emphasizing Type Four liberal social activism, and at the same time, preaching that Christ and the Spirit are divine principles working within and around us. Those seeking a personal relationship with Jesus as their Savior in the midst of a community charged with divine grace have therefore been finding Type Two emotional spirituality in a variety of nondenominational, fundamentalist, and charismatic settings.

Normative rabbinic Judaism has always stressed the religious expressions of Types One and Four: study of Jewish law and lore, three-times-daily recitation of a set liturgy, and observance through deeds of God's commands, the ethical and ritual *mitzvot*. Although aspects of Type Two religious enthusiasm, known in Hebrew as *hitlahavut*, are now making their way into the mainstream service, most of the twentieth century has witnessed a further growth of Type One spirituality. Conservative, Reform, and early Reconstructionist Judaism all emphasized decorum during worship and *Wissenschaft des Judentums,* the analytical approach to the study of Jewish texts as a means of demonstrating to the Western world the reasonableness and academic validity of Judaism's message.

Least pronounced within Judaism has been the spiritual inwardness of Type Three. This is due not only to Judaism's historical emphasis on the religious expressions of Types One and Four, but also because many of the European teachers of Jewish spiritual interiority perished during the Holocaust. Most who did survive have been reticent to spread their knowledge beyond select Orthodox circles due to traditional strictures concerning who is qualified to delve into kabbalah.

While the major religious traditions contain spiritual elements of each type, one or two of the types will be most pronounced in each faith. Therefore, if seekers are experiencing an imbalance or even a void in their spiritual lives, it is understandable that they would search for fulfillment in traditions that stress the spirituality of the quadrant diagonally opposite of where their own faith stands. Thus, Tilden Edwards, founding director of the Shalem Institute, offers the following advice to those seeking spiritual direction:

> Particular . . . faith traditions as expressed in a given place tend to emphasize certain paths more than others do, sometimes explicitly over others. If your tradition weights a particular path, that is fine, as long as it is truly yours.
>
> If it is not, and there is little room or understanding of the path you seem to be called to walk now, then you may have to find a spiritual companion from a more sympathetic tradition. . . .[13]

WHAT YOU MIGHT FIND

In Chapter 3 we discussed the sources and dynamics that shaped the approach to spiritual direction now prevalent in Roman Catholicism and Orthodox Christianity. Other historical faiths have their own traditions of guidance. While the relationship of guide to seeker is more often that of master to disciple than in the model drawn above, these also provide avenues to an inner awareness of the Divine.

While spiritual direction is in its infancy in liberal Judaism, two different movements help inform the Orthodox Jewish approach to guidance. One is Hasidism, founded in Eastern Europe around the teachings of Rabbi Israel Baal Shem Tov (d. 1759). *Mashpi'im* (spiritual prompters) serve the community by instructing newcomers in the Hasidic way of life and by guiding the more advanced in matters of study and observance and in questions of faith and religious insight on practical issues.

Of great importance is the occasional interview with the community's leader, who is known as the rebbe or *tzaddik* (righteous one). Different Hasidic groups refer to these interviews as *yechidut* (union), *pegishah* (meeting), or *bentchen zich* (to be blessed). Prior to the interview, the rebbe prepares himself by letting go of distractions and all previous concerns and by asking for divine guidance. The Hasid prepares himself by reflecting on his life and his receptivity to the rebbe as inspired leader and by writing a *kvittel,* a note expressing his particular concern. During the interview the rebbe will seek to intuitively link his soul through God with the soul of the Hasid. The rebbe will read the *kvittel,* question the Hasid, respond, and offer both *etzah* (insight) and a farewell blessing.

The rebbe, as the following story illustrates, most often uses the interview as an occasion to turn questions about the Hasid's prayer life or career into moments of spiritual deepening:

> A Hasid once came to the rebbe complaining that he found himself no longer able to study well. His prayers had become mechanical. The rebbe inquired of him where he resided (though he knew very well the circumstances of the Hasid's domicile). The Hasid replied that he lived in Byeshenkowitch. When the rebbe inquired where the Hasid did his business, the Hasid replied, "In Riga."
>
> "And how many months do you spend in Riga?" the rebbe queried. When the Hasid replied that he spent ten and a half months in Riga, the rebbe asked, "If you spend ten and a half months in Riga and only one and a half months in Byeshenkowitch, why do you say that you live in Byeshenkowitch?"
>
> "Rebbe," the Hasid replied, "In Riga I am for business, in Byeshenkowitch I am at home." And suddenly the Hasid understood the Rebbe's meaning. He had forsaken his domicile in Torah study and prayer and had taken up residence in business.[14]

The second influence on Orthodox Jewish spiritual guidance was the *musar* (moralist) movement of Rabbi Israel Salanter who lived in Lithuania and later Germany in the mid-nineteenth century. While valuing the intellectual study found in the yeshivot (Talmudic academies) he wished to attract the common people to Judaism by also stressing its emotional elements. To train spiritual leaders for the people, he had his disciples not only learn rabbinic legal texts but also study medieval ethical literature focusing on inner religious development. He devised an approach to spiritual friendship through which two companions would alternately help each other examine each other's intentions and deeds and to spur each on to greater growth. Salanter's influence is still felt today in yeshivot, which promote spiritual and study companionship *(hevruta),* and through the position of *yeshivah mashgiach,* a spiritual supervisor who provides individual guidance on matters of faith and practice and group direction through *shmoozim,* lectures on aspects of Judaism, observance, and the inner life.[15]

In Islam the most fundamental level of guidance is that of God to humanity. Divine revelation was channeled through the prophet Muhammad (d. 632 CE) and the Holy Koran, the word of Allah, God. To offer more detailed answers to the practical difficulties of everyday life the *shariah,* Islamic law, developed as "the way or road in the religion of Muhammad, which God has established for the guidance of God's people, both for the worship of God and for the duties of life."[16] This initial path to moral, religious development, called *muruwah,* is open to all believers.

The next two mystical stages of the journey to Allah, *futuwah* (spiritual chivalry) and *irfan* (knowledge of God), should not be undertaken without a true guide. Thus Sharafuddin Maneri, a Sufi sheikh who lived in fourteenth-century India, wrote:

> Remember, too, that an ordinary road is infested with thieves and robbers, so that one cannot travel along it without an escort. As for the mystic way, the world, one's ego, devils, men and *jinn* all infest this way, thus making it impossible to travel along it without an experienced holy man as one's escort. Remember, further, that there are many slippery places where it is easy to fall. Many philosophers and worldly minded people have become followers of their own base desires. They have gone without a perfect sheikh or

leader who has reached his goal on this way. ...
entered the wilderness where they fell and perished,
losing even their faith. In the course of his pilgrimage
a novice should expect to be assailed by spiritual crisis. Also, various types of mystical experiences might
occur: some might be satanic, others might be pro-
duced by his own ego, and still others could come
from the Merciful One Himself. This is entirely new to
the novice and he cannot discern the source of these
spiritual experiences. He needs the assistance of one
well versed in discerning these various spirits.[17]

The guide's relationship to the seeker on a personal
level is like that of Muhammad to the world, to bring
God's revelation. Minimally a sheikh would train a novice
for three years, employing various methods to help interpret and shape the disciple's inner states. Part of the training could include a forty-day retreat, called a *chilla,* and
teaching the disciple a method of invoking or chanting
God's names and qualities known as a *dhikr,* the remembrance of God. Ibn 'Abbad, who lived in Spain and Morocco
also during the fourteenth century, would assess his disciple's growth based on two criteria: *husn al-adab,* "proper demeanor," and *husn az-zann,* literally "thinking well of
God." These would lead to approaching all of life with
gratitude and clear inner vision, thus lessening the possibility for the most serious *shirk* (act of idolatry) the idolatry of egocentrism.[18]

Some sheikhs guide their disciples along an illumi-
native way, calling them to see all of creation miraculously
existing within God. Others lead seekers along a purga-
tive path, pointing to the Divine that is too often covered
by the mundane realities and desires of this world.[19] This
latter path was described by Bawa Muhaiyaddeen in his
book, *Sheikh and Disciple.* Among the images he employed

is one of the sheikh as a diamond cutter whose task it is to cut away flaws and to refine the facets of the gem that is the disciple's soul. Another of Bawa's metaphors is that of the sheikh as a mirror reflecting back to the disciple those defects that need to be cast away.[20]

When I asked Michael and Sarah exactly what Bawa had meant by these images, they offered these insights:

> MICHAEL: What did he mean by "cutting the gem?" Bawa was an iconoclast. He would zero in on whatever was your own personal idol and undo it. All the while beaming unconditional love, he would cut away at your most deeply embedded attachment, forcing you to consider what was really important in life.
>
> If you were a health-food fanatic he might serve you loaves of white bread at a meal. Once my brother came to visit with his militantly feminist significant other. Although I had never heard Bawa use these images before or since, that afternoon he offered teachings comparing a man's wife to a cow! Here he is joking about some hallowed truth-system you have structured your life around. You could hear the fuses blowing!
>
> While on the surface some of his instructions could be seen as contradictory, he would offer teachings individually designed to refine each disciples' personal imperfections.
>
> Bawa acknowledged that anything can be an icon. One of his disciples was a devout Muslim from the Middle East who seemed to be missing the universal spirit of Bawa's teaching of Islam. I remember one day in the course of answering some of his questions, (with only a translator and myself there) Bawa saying, almost as a throwaway, "Oh yes, the Koran is an exalted book—almost as exalted as the Bhagavad-Gita."
>
> This other guy was wound as tight as an alarm clock, actually almost scary. The part of Bawa's teaching that he heard was base-line faithful observance of Islamic practice. I never missed seeing him at morn-

ing prayers, and I also observed him over/a year slowly begin to lighten up.

Sometimes Bawa would use the "ricochet approach" by making a comment to another disciple that would cause you to think "that really wasn't meant for her—that insight was addressed to me." I myself experienced this on the second day of my initial visit with him. Speaking to another member of the group, Bawa said, "You can have a map, drive your car and still not get anywhere. For example, you could have read all the works of Ramakrishna (which I had) and still not know where you are going." I hadn't said anything about Ramakrishna. Intuitively, I knew he was talking to me and it was almost like an electric shock. No secrets!

Just by his being, Bawa could reflect to you whoever you needed him to be: father, mother, authority figure. In his loving, non-threatening reflection you could work through past issues, seeing both your contradictions and your potential mirrored back.

SARAH: Given my personality type, I can be prone to melancholy and am quite sensitive to criticism. One day Bawa cut away my whole identification with sadness just by saying, "Sarah, if you're happy, I'm happy." On another occasion a large gathering had come to hear him speak and I was charged with distributing fruit. Bawa criticized my every move. It went on and on and on until I finally saw how absurd the criticism was. I realized "this is a saturation exercise," and at that moment I began to confront the over-sensitivity that had plagued me for so long. When Bawa saw that I had understood the point and stopped being reactive to the criticism, he stopped and he gave me a sweet smile.

Beatrice Bruteau is one of today's innovative spiritual teachers. Her works include *Radical Optimism* (1994) and *God's Ecstasy: The Creation of a Self-Creating World*

(1997). Among the influences she considers most forma-
tive to her religious views were two years spent in spiritual guidance at the Vedanta (Hindu) Center in New York
City. Living in Jefferson City, Missouri, in the 1930s,
Beatrice's parents disaffiliated from their local Southern Baptist church, put off by what they felt was an anti-
intellectual bias. As a young girl, Beatrice found meaning
in classical music, science, and philosophy, particularly
Plato's *Phaedrus,* which speaks of a heavenly ascent and
vision of eternal realities. However, her greatest early
inspiration came from experiences with nature.

> I spent a lot of my childhood alone in a wonderful
> backyard (I still value being alone). I watched clouds,
> I climbed trees, I sat in bowers of blossoms. I espe-
> cially liked swinging and singing. I danced in the
> moonlight and enjoyed thunderstorms. My father
> taught me flowers and my mother taught me stars.
> From the very beginning I felt the presence of divine
> nature, a personal reality pervading everything. I had
> many experiences of exaltation.

Her first introduction to Asian tradition came at age
fourteen when she read Lin Yutang's *Wisdom of China and
India.* During her high-school years she was moved by the
writings of Khalil Gibran and Omar Khayyam and, most
of all, by the unabridged dictionary's long paragraph on
pantheism. While an undergraduate at the University of
Kansas City (now the University of Missouri) studying
mathematics and physics, she became a humanist
Unitarian for two years. In the end though, she felt that
something was missing, something transcendent and
divine, something to worship in awe, something to reach
in an elevated state.

A sequence of accidents led to the answer. On the eve of leaving Missouri to take up a graduate fellowship at the University of Pittsburgh, an idle perusal of a book rack gave her L. L. Whyte's *The Next Development in Man*. This then led to the chance discovery in Pittsburgh's Carnegie Library of Romain Rolland's book, *Prophets of New India,* and biographies of Sri Ramakrishna (1836–1886) and his disciple, Swami Vivekananda, who brought Vedanta to the United States in 1893 for the first Parliament of the World's Religions.

> My meeting with Sri Ramakrishna was the big spiritual moment of my life. Everything I have done since has grown out of that. God is real and God can be realized, actually experienced. There are spiritual practices that prepare one for that experience. Reality is One—various human traditions describe it in different ways. All these ways bring devotees to the goal. The One Reality, Brahman, is nondual—it is both formless (infinite) and expressing in multitudinous forms (finite). It plays as World and we delight in It. This is what I still believe.

Ideas that also proved to interest Beatrice were *samsara,* the eternal cycle of birth, growth, decay, death, and rebirth; *karma,* the positive and negative value our actions have in determining the value of this life and next; and *moksha,* release from life's cycle to be reabsorbed into the One. Also interesting was the notion that one could gain *darshan,* insight, by relationship with a guru, a realized soul radiating the Divine, who can guide you to a sense of the sacred both through meditative practice and through everyday tasks.

After completing a master's degree in mathematics and taking another year in philosophy, Beatrice moved to New York City, joined the Vedanta Center, and enjoyed an intense life built around the center on West 71st Street. Beatrice described her two years of guidance at the Vedanta Center in this way:

> Our experience at the center encompassed an entire lifestyle. When newcomers arrived they were asked to select an *ishta,* an aspect of Divinity that most appealed to them. Personally, I was drawn to the idea of the Divine as Absolute. Three times a day we meditated and three times a week we attended public lectures. During our private interviews with the swami we were asked about our meditation and instructed as to what forms it should take.
>
> Each day we were responsible for polishing the wood in the center, placing flowers on the altar, preparing meals and taking care of transportation issues. Through our routine we each were to continually repeat our own mantra, that word or verse given to each of us by the swami, reflecting our own spiritual needs. Because I wasn't ready to settle in and be initiated I didn't choose to receive a mantra of my own.

About this time (1952) another chain of accidents led to a further development. The *New York Times Book Review* presented a biography of Edith Stein, the German philosopher of Jewish birth who became a Carmelite nun and died in Auschwitz. The book itself, read aloud to a blind friend, led to Beatrice accompanying the friend to Columbia University to finish her Ph.D. in philosophy under the mentorship of Daniel Walsh and to the auditing of Walsh's courses in medieval Catholic philosophy. A chance meeting with a Dominican priest sent Beatrice on to Fordham University to study Catholic philosophy. The Jesuits took a kind interest in her eagerness to learn and soon she was both studying and working at the university, where she remained until 1967.

What is the difference between Hinduism and Buddhism? I once heard the following description: For the Hindu reality equals the world plus One, Brahman, the divine; for the Buddhist reality equals the world and nothing more. Buddhism, a nontheistic tradition, is based on the Four Noble Truths: All of life is suffering; suffering arises from craving and desire; to stop suffering one must stop one's craving; the means to do so is through following the Noble Eightfold Path—Right Views, Right Resolve, Right Speech, Right Conduct, Right Livelihood, Right Effort, Right Mindfulness and Right Concentration.[21]

Fundamental to all forms of Buddhism is the principle that we never perceive anything as it really is.[22] Even if our organs of perception function properly, our attachment or aversion to the stimuli we perceive can distort our true understanding of the world. Different movements within Buddhism have developed various meditative techniques to help seekers deal with these distortions:

- *samatha*—meditation that focuses concentration on a single point. If you are concentrating on following the rising and falling of your breath, when thoughts occur you simply let them go rather than analyze or dwell on them
- *vipassana*—insight meditation that broadens the field of attention to include our thoughts, emotions, and bodily sensations. In this meditation you note the content of the experience before letting it go. For example, if you are concentrating on following your breathing pattern and a feeling of anxiety arises, you might note it by whispering to yourself mentally, "anxiety, anxiety," and then let the thought go.

These forms of meditation described briefly above help the seeker realize that there is no essential "I" behind our thoughts and emotions, that we are not our instincts, not our feelings, and not our thoughts. We can become aware of when and how our feelings and thoughts arise, note them, and not be automatically carried away by them. This practice of mindfulness can lead to greater serenity and balance in our lives as well as an appreciation of the blessings and possibilities present in each moment.

Within the Zen tradition as developed in China, Korea, and Japan, other forms of practice include:

- *zazen*—an extended form of sitting meditation that focuses on proper posture, sitting, and breathing. With great patience the disciple works through all feelings and discomforts that might arise during the sitting to achieve peacefulness and freedom from all attachments.
- *koan practice*—the use of puzzling, paradoxical, or even nonsensical statements that challenge the limits of the problem-solving intellect, pushing the student beyond the bounds of cognitive reason to reach enlightenment.

The object of both types of practice is to shake the seeker out of everyday awareness and ultimately to induce an indescribable experience of illumination called *nirvana* or *satori*. An example of how a *koan* can be used to burst through the ordinary boundaries of cognition can be found in this interaction between a female disciple and the great Zen master Hakuin (d. 1768 CE).

"What is the sound of one hand?" he asked her.
"Much better than hearing the sound of Hakuin's hand is to clap both hands—then we can do business," she shot back.

Hakuin replied, "If you can really do business by clapping both hands, you don't need to hear the sound of one hand."[23]

At one time, when seekers first came for guidance, they were shown correct posture and breathing techniques and then told to just begin their sitting meditation and "let your thoughts go." Mentoring and more explicit direction seemed reserved for those who persevered and showed seriousness by wanting to become nuns or monks. One seeker actually told me that his initial guidance amounted to "take this cushion and sit on it for fourteen hours."

However, current Buddhist teachers, particularly in the West, use a lighter touch, even using humor in discussing seekers' questions such as, "What is mindfulness?" or "How can one be fully present in the moment?"

Different gradations of the relationship exist. The guru/disciple model does continue in which the seeker submits all aspects of his or her life to the master's direction. Other levels of guidance can include relationship with a *kalyanamitra*, a "friend of the heart, " in the mutuality of spiritual companionship. The teacher-student relationship is more permanent and directed and becomes formalized by the student's request for instruction.

———————————

———————————————

5

BLESSINGS AND DRAWBACKS

BENEFITS OF SPIRITUAL DIRECTION

What might the seeker derive from interfaith spiritual direction? On a basic level the same blessings and grace that can be gained from any fitting seeker-guide relationship. Some respondents offered these observations on how spiritual direction made their lives richer:

"I learned that God can be personal and that I can relate to God in an intimate way. . . ."

"I gained a 'friend along the way' to mirror for me my distortions and missteps, as well as see things from a vantage point that I can't."

As my own journey of guidance with the Cenacle Sisters has progressed I have noticed that some aspects of the spiritual movement described at the end of Chapter 3 have begun to unfold in my own life. A variation of a verse in the psalms kept repeating itself in my head, "No—I shall die to live and recount the works of the Lord."[1] This signaled to me that certain aspects of my life had begun to pass away while other, newer features were coming to be. Material possessions, communal office, and professional recognition, once so important to me, no longer seemed that important. For the first time I found myself able to be alone, and I began to look forward to silent retreat, something that was unthinkable for me before. I saw my impatience and judgmental attitudes begin to decrease as a new sense of understanding and even empathy began to grow. I began to see a transcendent purpose to my move from Fort Lauderdale to Philadelphia, as if I had been called into new relationships and new opportunities for growth, even when those came in response to painful experiences. I knew I was becoming "other" when I would leave a hospital room or a house of mourning and hear myself thanking God for the chance to extend God's care to those who needed it most.

History and personal testimony confirm that the inner qualities of wholeness, peace and clarity, tenderness, joy, and feeling empowered to move forward in the face of fear can blossom from any truly positive bond of spiritual direction. However, interfaith spiritual direction offers a unique gift. It allows a liberation of the soul as the divine moves through the seeker's life. By this I am not referring to seekers totally casting off the rules and beliefs of their own faith. Rather, when the guide and seeker are of different traditions and bring no agendas to the relationship other than mutual respect and bearing witness to God working in our lives, something singularly grace-filled can occur. As one seeker put it, "You can become, I think, more of a convert to God than to any particular faith system." Because the seeker is not bound by the rules of the guide's faith, neither has to be concerned about heresy or breaking the religious law of either faith. Instead the guide can help the seeker detect the movement of the spirit in his or her life and allow that person the freedom to draw connections to their professed religious tradition.[2]

Another great blessing of interfaith spiritual direction can be found when the seeker draws those connections between the insights of their guide's faith and their own. Being exposed, perhaps for the first time, to aspects of spirituality from quadrants other than those stressed by the seeker's tradition can lead to fresh and vital insights. Respondents from all traditions cite this as being essential in transforming their understanding of their own faith.

Dr. Hillevi Ruumet, a transpersonal psychologist and spiritual director now residing in southern Oregon, described how guidance in another tradition literally rescued her Christian faith:

> If not for Buddhism I would have never understood the deeper mystical teachings of Christianity, and probably would have continued to throw out the "baby" (the original essential teachings of Jesus and his early disciples) with the "bathwater" (patriarchal, power-oriented church structure and dogma).

Bob, the spiritual director from Rochester we met in Chapter 4, received guidance and advanced training in both the Korean and Tibetan Buddhist traditions. He now brings methods from these schools to help his seekers attain a more profound understanding of Jesus' life and his parables.

There is a lot of story and narrative in scripture. Viewing them as *koans* can help Christians in the West go beyond the surface of scripture and connect directly with their divine lineage. In this way the text can come alive.

Emulating the engagement of a Zen master and disciple, I ask seekers to reflect for long periods on certain tales. A favorite is John 8, where an adulteress is brought before Jesus. The crowd demands that the sentence of stoning be passed. Jesus speaks and then scribbles in the dust, "Whoever is without sin cast the first stone." Slowly the accusers disappear, one by one. Rather than analyze the text I ask them to ponder the question, "What did Jesus write on the ground?" Like a *koan* it bursts the bounds of their intellect and reason and allows God's message contained for them in the story to break through.

When I asked Beatrice Bruteau if there was any particular reason why she had left the Vedanta Center she looked at me and said, "I never left Vedanta—I took it with me." She explained Vedanta to her new Catholic friends and teachers and interpreted Christian images and ideas in Vedantic ways. Her doctoral dissertation in philosophy (at Fordham) was on Sri Aurobindo, a twentieth-century Vedantic yogin and philosopher who stressed the reality and worthiness of the world as God's self-expression. Having been helped greatly by several Catholic spiritual directors, Beatrice began to practice as a spiritual director and retreat guide, mingling experiences from both traditions. One of the numerous examples of how this creative cross-fertilization shows in Beatrice's spiritual teaching is expressed in this excerpt from her 1996 book, *What We Can Learn from the East*. It describes the movement of prayer as twofold: communion with God followed by having God's goodness act through you.

In the case of the life of prayer, *insight* refers to the goal that is expressed as "knowing and loving God" or "seeing the truth" or "being enlightened" or "realizing the Ultimate." The Journey to insight is often regarded as a passage from the unreal to the Real, from *samsara* to *nirvana,* from the many to the One. *Manifestation* on the other hand bespeaks a movement in the opposite direction. The subject has the experience of being the author and origin of some reality and of projecting it outward. . . .

Now it seems to me that very often the spiritual life, where it is studied as the mystical life, as distinguished from the moral or religious life (concerned with creed, code, and cult), has been presented as a matter only of attaining insight. All our efforts are directed to leaving this multiform world and cleaving to the One God.

But once one is so united with God, then what? Usually this is considered the end of the story: the prince and princess are wed and live happily ever after. I have heard that Swami Brahmananda said, "spiritual life *begins with samadhi.*" In a Christian context one would say, if one is united with God, then one must do what God does, and what God does is to be endlessly self-expressive (as well as self-uniting) in the Trinity, and create the world (worlds).[3]

For Deborah Ann, interfaith spiritual direction actually opened new gateways back to Judaism.

More than anything else, it [spiritual direction] helps me to see God as the process of the Living God continually creating itself, if you will, through us. And it has helped me to appreciate how I define being a Jew, which has freed me more than anything else to start my formal Jewish education and to take on more aspects of Judaism. . . .

I became a Jew when I became a person of faith—faith with a small *f.* . . .

Now I see Judaism as a beautiful, nuanced, wise, and moving way to express my love for God (when I'm not still seeing some of those pesky rules as arbitrary, rigid, and inconvenient) . . . but I love my Friday night candle lighting. I had expected the synagogue to bring God to me. Now I walk in (more frequently than I used to) and bring God with me.

For me, one of interfaith spiritual direction's greatest gifts has been the opportunity to discover aspects in my own tradition that I had known only intellectually or not at all. Having studied concepts like *penimiyut* (inwardness) with no practice to nurture it was like being blind and hearing someone tell me about the color chartreuse. It was only when my first spiritual director, Sister Elizabeth Hilman, introduced me to some simple spiritual practices I had not known that the concept of *penimiyut* became a reality. She told me to select a biblical verse—anything that immediately came to mind and that seemed to rise from my heart. I was to find a quiet place, sit straight, relaxed but alert, and recite my verse slowly for ten minutes each day. Feeling as if I was resting in God's tender hands, I was to let my other concerns go. Even if I didn't recognize it immediately, blessings would accrue if I just showed up faithfully day after day.

These simple instructions not only began a process that helped change my life—they opened for me previously closed veins of Jewish spiritual treasure. The verse that I chose (or, perhaps, that chose me) was "The Lord is near to the brokenhearted and will redeem those crushed of spirit."[4] Within a few weeks some rather amazing things began to occur. During my meditation this verse, which I recited in Hebrew, began to reformulate itself in my mind, revealing whole new realms of meaning.

The Hebrew word for near, *karov,* connotes close-ness, drawing near, offering a sacrifice, and engaging in battle. Suddenly I found myself asking God to draw near and break open my closed heart so I might be closer to God. I found myself asking God to help me engage in the battle to shatter the arrogance and presumptuousness of my heart so that I could make room for others and for God. I found myself asking God to accept the offering of my bro-ken heart as God did the sacrifices in Solomon's Temple so that I could experience God's redeeming presence.

Prompted by curiosity I decided to investigate whether my experiences were analogous to elements found within Jewish tradition. I discovered that the repe-tition of a sacred verse, known in Hebrew as *gerushin,* was a common practice of kabbalah and Hasidism.[5] Mystically inclined rabbinic scholars would commit sec-tions of the Talmud to memory and repeat them over and over again. Through this mantra-style meditation new understandings and interpretations of these legal texts would unfold. When faced with choices between two legitimate rabbinic legal opinions, certain figures would bring these questions into their meditations to gain insight as to which course of action they should pursue.[6]

As my months of spiritual direction and meditation continued I began to understand other aspects of Judaism in a deeper way as well. To engage in kabbalah the seek-er was required to be at least forty years old and to have a solid grounding in Jewish law and lore.[7] It seems that these prescriptions were set to ensure the emotional maturity of the prospective mystic and to prevent heresy. Yet my own experience suggested that true openness to God might only come after having undergone some loss and reversal in one's life, events that usually occur around middle age. Stripped of any illusions of self-sufficiency or immortality, we might then be more receptive to the Divine Spirit moving within us.

You need not have an extensive religious background to enjoy the benefits of spiritual direction and personal prayer. Some seekers, like Michael in Chapter 4 and Geoff, whom we will meet in Chapter 8, actually had no formal religious training and yet have gained much from spiritual guidance. However, my own experiences gave me a new appreciation for the rule that one engaging in kabbalah should be trained in Judaism's classical texts. The unfolding of other prayer verses revealing new realms of meaning has happened to me again and again. Sometimes I feel addressed by words from our scripture or liturgy, as if God is speaking to me through this conversation of passages. Sharing these experiences monthly with my spiritual director has helped reveal the hidden ways that God is acting in my life. It is only now that I feel I deeply understand the purpose of my previous years of Jewish study.

SOME OF THE PITFALLS

While there is much to be gained from interfaith spiritual direction, the experience is not without its problems. One obstacle along the way might be a lack of understanding or even resistance to your quest by religious leaders and friends from your own denomination. At the August 1999 "Christ and the Buddha" conference in Burlingame, California, participants who have gained guidance and inspiration from certain Buddhist practices spoke of their struggle to remain authentically Christian and of the concerns expressed to them by their home clergy. Dave, an editor from New England, described his personal experience this way:

I didn't really ever "decide" to begin seeking spiritual direction outside my faith, it just happened fairly naturally on its own at one point—with some difficult consequences.

As a teenager I was fascinated be religion of all kinds, and my interest in Buddhism goes back to that time. I came into the Eastern Orthodox Church as a young man living in Alaska, where I had spent four years in the Coast Guard, and several more years as a civilian. The Church became the structure of my whole life—and that has never changed fundamentally. It was easy, especially in the first years, to concentrate my reading and practice to Orthodox Christianity since it was such a rich tradition. There was so much for me to learn.

However, as years went by, my natural interest in all the different ways that people had approached the truth re-arose. I continued to do a lot of reading in other faiths. I had an aversion to people "mixing and matching" spiritual traditions according to their own desires, so I limited my experience to reading. But one of the results of this reading was a great love and respect for the Buddhist traditions.

By the time I was in my forties I felt, for the first time, a need to distance myself from the Church a bit. This may have been part of a mid-life crisis, except that it didn't feel like a crisis. I spent three months without going to any Church service. It was during this time that whatever interior barrier had kept me from Buddhist practice came tumbling down. I think it may have been that I had finally come to the point of trusting myself, and that I had the time. So I went to a meditation class at a local Zen center. From the first time that I sat I knew that I would be involved with this practice for a long time.

I returned to church three months later with my sitting meditation practice firmly established. My parish priest, whom I had known for twenty years, was not thrilled with this. I was open about it but Father John didn't seem to want to say much about it.

I'm pretty sure he thought it was a phase that I would outgrow, and he probably thought it would only drive me away if he "commanded" me to give up the practice. There were a couple of difficult years. Though he wasn't talking to me about my Buddhist connection, he was mentioning "other religions" sometimes in sermons and indicating that we had no need for them.

I hadn't planned to do anything but meditation, but since I didn't meditate with other Buddhist groups on a regular basis, it felt good to sometimes sit with other people. Being in these sitting groups led to going to talks and to being exposed to Buddhist teaching. I felt the need to talk to someone who used the vocabulary of Buddhism, since what was happening to me was hard to express without that language. I began to interview with teachers of Zen and Vipassana traditions.

An interesting thing began to happen to Father John—he was opening up a bit to the fact that I was finding something very true and important in Buddhist practice. I believe this came about because I didn't buckle under to his unexpressed but unmistakable preference that I abandon it. But it also came about because I continued my contact with him as my spiritual father. As I continued to go to him for the sacrament of confession, I believe he saw that Buddhism was leading me closer to God, and it was certainly not leading me away from the church.

I believe I am fortunate to have a parish priest capable of coming around the way that Father John did. I don't think there are a huge number of Orthodox priests around today who would be able to make such a change. I also feel that it was very important that I stood my ground and didn't give up on him either—it certainly was a matter of years before there was much understanding. But it happened.

Dave was fortunate. Not only Orthodox priests, but also clergy from many religious traditions oppose what they see as inauthentic "spiritual hybridism." Rabbi Jerome Epstein, chief executive officer of the United Synagogue of Conservative Judaism, voiced such sentiment when he stated, "It's not okay to be a Jew and a Protestant or a Jew and a Catholic. And it's not okay to be a Jew and a Buddhist."[8]

Another potential obstacle along the path of interfaith spiritual direction is the fit between the guide and seeker. Depending on the seeker's current needs the direction relationship, be it same-faith or cross-faith, can be undermined if the guide is too directive or too laissez-faire, too similar to the seeker in spiritual temperament or not understanding enough, too off-putting or too chummy.

Rose Mary Dougherty, a member of the School Sisters of Notre Dame and Program Director at Shalem, tells how one of her own former spiritual directors became so empathetic that their guidance relationship could not continue because it became too much of a friendship. Another director's spiritual journey was so similar to Rose Mary's that they wound up sharing many inspiring conversations but lost focus on God's presence in Rose Mary's life, the *raison d'être* of spiritual direction. Her conclusion: "Eventually I came to realize that it didn't matter if my director was a man or a woman, married or single, a person of the same denomination or different. What mattered was that those involved were responding to an invitation from God to be together and that we trusted God's presence in our response more than we trusted ourselves."[9]

What also matters is a clear understanding on the part of both seeker and guide concerning the type of counsel the seeker is or should be seeking. In his most influential paper, "A Theory of Motivation," the noted psychologist Abraham Maslow proposed that human beings have a hierarchy of needs. Stated simply, the first level consists of our physiological needs such as food and shelter, which ensure our survival. Once those have been met, our need for safety, acceptance, and approval—our "belongingness" needs—emerge. If these are not fulfilled we can evince symptoms of fear, insecurity, selfishness, and anxiety. Only when these needs have been reasonably met can people tap into a giving sense of "metamotivation that is passionate, selfless and profound," whose empathy and generosity can allow one to transcend the distinction between "self" and "not-self."[10]

Often people seek direction when they might, on a more fundamental level, need therapy more. Hillevi Ruumet, who is both a spiritual guide and a licensed psychologist, put it best: "Sometimes people seek spiritual direction when they really need psychological counseling because they find it more 'acceptable.' That wouldn't rule them out, but I would have to be clear about what my role is."

In same-faith relationships this problem can be difficult enough if the guide isn't clear about his or her role. In interfaith settings the problem can be amplified if the guide feels that religious practice or doctrine or discerning providential meaning can transcend all unresolved problems and even make them disappear. Indeed, American Buddhist teachers differ on this very issue. Some advocate the classical Buddhist teaching of "letting go of everything" so as not to identify with any state whatsoever. Others see engaging and resolving issues of personality as being as critical as meditation in the quest for a complete life.[11] One Buddhist teacher who seems to favor the latter view told me, "The Buddha never dealt with issues like self-loathing that many seekers in the West face today."

Even more difficult is the seeker not recognizing or, worse, denying the type of counseling they really need. Because the guide's faith can seem exotic and even other-worldly, there is a real danger that its fresh insights might appear to the seeker as the absolute in divine revelation. Seekers might fall prey to believing that they have found the magic elixir to cure all problems, particularly if the guide or other seekers encourage that view. While the same unresolved emotional issues usually raise their ugly heads—perhaps in a new guise—during or after the first rush of zeal, it is possible for them to remain unrecognized or denied and, therefore, untreated or even exacerbated. As one observer bluntly stated about some in his circle who sought guidance from an Asian spiritual leader during the seventies without facing their own emotional issues, "there was a lot of craziness going on."

Another matter of grave concern is the over-susceptibility of the seeker to the authority and directives of the guide. As previously noted, seekers usually first pursue guidance at critical junctures in their lives: following a loss, when faced with a major decision or the possibility of upheaval, or when experiencing a crisis of belief. These are especially vulnerable moments. If a guide mistakes his or her symbolic role of helping to identify the Divine in a seeker's life and instead identifies him or herself as the Divine in a seeker's life, then the situation becomes ripe for abuse.

Sarah's account of the exploits of the Philadelphia "guru cartel" in Chapter 2 graphically describes what can happen when guides consider themselves to be incarnations of the Divine rather than those whose right conduct should reflect the Divine. The emotional fragility of some seekers combined with an attraction to bond with a person they perceive (and who might very well be portrayed) as one who embodies sacred power can prove both overwhelming and traumatic. During the 1980s and 90s sexual scandals did occur within American Buddhism.[12] The possibility for such abuse exists in almost any spiritual direction setting. This is why the most experienced spiritual directors counsel seekers to select guidance situations that will minimize the potential for sexual attraction.[13] That potential can be dangerously increased in interfaith relationships when the guide's tradition ascribes to such mentors special sanctity and power and when the guide might appear to the seeker to be coming from the "other world" because his or her dress and demeanor come from another culture.

Sexual boundaries are not the only lines in danger of being crossed. Personal religious boundaries might be at risk as well. I have been fortunate to have two wonderful spiritual directors, Sister Elizabeth Hilman and Sister Barbara Whittemore. Our relationships, in Florida and now New Jersey, have opened new vistas for sharing our traditions and recognizing God's working in my life. When I first called I clearly indicated that I was seeking spiritual direction as a non-Christian and that has always been respected. However, not all spiritual friendships are so blessed.

Some time ago a Jewish woman came to see me quite distraught. For seven years she had studied and received spiritual direction from a Christian cabalist in the Philadelphia area.[14] The woman felt that her mentor was not only a guide but also a personal friend. However, discord developed when the woman began to question the legitimacy of her guide's Christian appropriation of Jewish mysticism, particularly the identifying of the feminine, imminent aspect of God, *Shechinah,* with the Virgin Mary. The guide then informed her directee that she, the guide, was directly reflecting the light of God's knowledge to others and that doubt was tantamount to heresy. She also indicated that if this woman did not continue her studies she would go mad. The woman was saddened but relieved when I confirmed her intuition that spiritual direction is not jail, and that she should leave this situation in favor of a healthier, less presumptuous one.

While this example is extreme, there is always the possibility that one committed to his or her own faith will make an overture of conversion. When attending a training program for contemplative group leaders sponsored by the Shalem Institute, I observed an Episcopal service held that Sunday morning. One of my fellow students approached me as I was sitting outside the circle of worshippers considering the points of commonality and difference between their service and my own.

"Howard," he asked, "why don't you join the circle?"

"I don't feel that I can, with everyone affirming their belief in Jesus as part of the service."

"Well," responded my friend, "did you ever consider becoming baptized?"

Well, no, but this interchange points out how even a well-intended discussion might inadvertently cross the boundary between sharing and proselytizing.

This boundary can become even weaker when the guide was raised in the seeker's faith but converted from it to another tradition. If the guide has not resolved his or her own feelings about their former religion they can easily counter-transfer those feelings onto the seeker. Derision of the seeker's faith might occur consciously or even inadvertently. The guide might openly urge or gently nudge the seeker to convert, not because the spirit is actually moving the seeker in that direction but to validate the guide's own life choices. One American Buddhist teacher quietly told me that some of her colleagues would even mock dedicated fellow teachers who have impeccable credentials but still show some interest in their former traditions.

Conversely, the individual who enters into a relationship of interfaith spiritual direction must be clear about what he or she desires. Exploring conversion is one thing; seeking guidance from another religious perspective is something else. The insights of a warm, wise director from another faith might lead the seeker to assume that no analogous wisdom or practice can be found in his or her religion. The seeker shouldn't jump to the conclusion that conversion is the only path to spiritual growth. Instead the seeker might first search for corresponding ideas in his or her own faith or try to understand why it takes a different point of view. Consultation with a teacher from one's own faith or an adult study program in one's own faith might prove helpful.

Differences in culture can also provide an impediment to fulfilling interfaith guidance relationships. Almost every seeker and guide with whom I have corresponded has cited variances in customs and language as being a real difficulty. Sarah and Michael each love and honor Bawa Muhaiyaddeen. Yet in describing the cultural differences between his Sri Lankan background and her American orientation, Sarah said it was necessary to use discriminatory wisdom. "Bawa himself said that we must sift every word that comes from the mouth of the sheikh. This is even more true when the seeker is relying on a translator, as I was. But in another sense, Bawa communicated very clearly on a different level—a level beyond language and cultural differences." Michael also felt that you had to sort out what was essence and what was cultural.

Deborah Ann, who prizes her interfaith guidance relationship, did experience some cultural resistance as an American Jew seeking guidance in another Western faith, Christianity. Some of that resistance was internal: What was she, a nice Jewish girl, doing among these Christians? What might they have in store for her? Might her experience lead her to value Jewish tradition less? She relates that other obstacles were, however, objective in nature:

> Drawbacks? Language was certainly a big one. Even the same words—like *grace, spirit, discernment*—can have different meaning for people with different religious experiences. Benefit does come when I can be comfortable with what I can't understand, when I can hold it within me open to the possibility of understanding.

While ours is an era of great interfaith tolerance and exchange, we cannot ignore the history of competition, animosity, and even active persecution that has marked the relationships of the world's religions. The life-enhancing symbols of one faith may well conjure up memories of forced expulsions, conversions, and bloodshed for members of another. Prejudicial ideas long embedded in biblical texts and sacred rites may no longer even be recognized as being hostile to another religion.

Such was my experience at an interdenominational spirituality seminar in February 1995. One of the ministers who was acting as a guide during that week organized a dramatic reenactment of a Gospel scene. Jesus had come to a synagogue one Sabbath and was approached by an ailing woman. When he attempted to heal her the elders of the congregation tried to stop him, indicating that petitionary prayers for healing were prohibited on the Jewish Sabbath. Over the protestations of the elders, the congregation urged Jesus on and he healed the woman.

Since I often find myself a minority of one at such gatherings, I expect my colleagues to worship in the name of Jesus (as long as they don't expect me to). I do not want us to homogenize our religious expressions to the point where they reflect none of our particularity and become meaningless. However, when I saw those playing the synagogue elders pushing down the woman that Jesus was trying to raise, I simply had to pull back and leave. Of all the miracles ascribed to Jesus, why, I wondered, did they have to pick one that demeaned my faith?

The exchange that took place the next morning helps illuminate both the drawbacks and the benefits that such interactions can bring. I met privately with the guide and voiced my dismay about the drama and my doubts about the historical validity of the scene. While petitionary prayer is generally not recited on the Sabbath, we do offer prayers for healing, and a major Jewish principle from the second century BCE indicates that the saving of lives pushes aside any strictures of our Sabbath. The guide told me that he had chosen that scene because it symbolized to him the plight of a woman within his denomination whose initiatives were being suppressed by members of his church's hierarchy. I informed him that his explanation actually made matters worse because he was identifying the heavy-handed denomination officials as Jews who were putting down the true healing work of Jesus in his church. While we reached some personal accord, I told him that my trust had been broken and I could no longer be involved in group sessions where he was offering guidance or coordinating worship.

My colleagues at the seminar were wonderfully supportive. While I did not want to make an issue of the matter, they felt that they needed to discover how God's spirit was moving them as Christians. We talked about how this incident was calling us to greater sensitivity toward each other's traditions, toward greater mutual respect. Our group and individual exchanges actually brought us to a greater understanding and closeness as God's people than we had experienced before.

THE EXPERIENCE OF BEING A GUIDE

Most of the observations above have come from the perspective of the seekers. But how do those who act as interfaith spiritual guides view the experience? Just as Dave met resistance as an interfaith seeker, so have some interfaith guides experienced opposition from their own denominations. Dr. Mary Ann Woodman of the Center for Spiritual Practice has a full-time guidance practice with five offices in Oregon, and California. While sixty percent of her seekers are Christian, she also guides Sufis, Buddhists, Hindus, and Jews. Formed in the Roman Catholic tradition, she was first introduced to interfaith spirituality in the sixties and has been an active participant in the Ashland, Oregon, Interfaith Ministers Association for twelve years. Mary Ann speaks of having learned the "spiritual tools" of various traditions. Yet she remains firmly rooted in Christianity, feeling that those who selectively appropriate practices from here and there wind up with a faith life "like a cut bouquet, beautiful—but without roots and ungrounded, ultimately fated to wither." Despite her training and commitment she has felt shunned by members of her own church community for her more universal approach. For Mary Ann, universal brings the essential quality of catholicity to her ministry.

Dale Rhodes, Radha's spiritual guide from Chapter 4, identifies with Unitarian Universalism and is one of seven guides at the Interfaith Spiritual Center in Portland, Oregon. Opened in November 1998 under the leadership of Sister Cecilia Ranger, the I.S.C. has guides from all of the major traditions and is truly cross-denominational in those whom they serve and companion. Dale's own seekers include Hindus, Muslims, and one avowed Pagan. Recently interracial, interfaith couples have been seeking him out in their attempts to discern how God might be manifest in their marriages and family life.

The Spiritual Directors International, headquartered in San Francisco, sponsors an e-group through which spiritual directors can go on-line to discuss various issues including peer support, recommendations concerning current and potential seekers, and suggested readings. In September 1999, Dale joined the e-mail discussion, mentioning that he was reading a book on Judaism by Rabbi Wayne Dosick, *Dancing with God,* and asking for recommendations from other interfaith spiritual directors. While he received expressions of support from guides who have been involved in Christian-Buddhist dialogue, at least five to seven respondents challenged his core assumptions. How, they asked, can you offer guidance to someone of a different denomination or tradition and, how can you offer guidance without trying to lead people to Jesus? As a result of this interchange, Dale sometimes wonders if it will be easier for him to be accepted by his colleagues as an openly gay spiritual director rather than as an openly interfaith director!

The question of cultural difference arises for the guides just as it does for interfaith seekers. Hillevi describes the dynamics this way:

> It does matter that these teachings and practices fit who we are psychologically and culturally. For example, I have learned and experienced so much through Tibetan Buddhism, and feel enormous respect and gratitude for my teachers. But on the practical, experiential level much felt culturally foreign to me. The inner symbols that arose spontaneously were still mostly Christian. Now I know that there was a message in that.

Even when the seekers come from the same cultural milieu, matters of translating terms and checking one's assumptions still can exist. One Jewish spiritual guide claimed that there really is no difference between the guidance she offers to fellow Jews and that which she offers to others, with one possible exception. With fellow Jews she can sometimes use "shorthand" when referring to certain terms, concepts, and stories. With her non-Jewish seekers she must remember to interpret or explain.

Not all interfaith guides see so little difference between the direction they offer to those of their own tradition and to those who come from other traditions. Another Jewish guide, the one described previously who offers direction to military personnel, takes a different approach. When Jews come to see him for guidance, he tries to bring them into fuller appreciation of a Jewish spiritual path. With non-Jewish seekers he tries to help them explore what their own spirited path might be and create the inner space needed for such an exploration.

When it comes to matters of discerning whether to enter into a guidance relationship with a seeker from another faith, questions of mutual religious understanding do play a role.

> Do they need me to be dogmatically on the same wavelength? Can I share that world enough to work within it if they need me to? Do I have enough knowledge to do that? The more dogmatic and denominationally based the person's need, the less I see myself as right for them.

While matters of culture, terminology, and doctrine do come into play, most directors indicate that the criteria for a good guidance relationship cut across faith boundaries.

> - Do I feel that this is a good connection?
> - Is there trust?
> - Do I feel that spiritual direction is really what this person is asking of me?
> - Do I sense anything in myself that might get in the way of my ability to be fully open and present?
> - If so, can I get past it?

Rose Mary Dougherty expresses her path of discernment this way:

> Do I have the interior freedom to listen to them without putting my agenda on them? Can I be open to God? Can I be in a prayerful place with them or am I being pulled away?
>
> I can't be in direction with everyone. Sometimes I feel less comfortable with a person from my own tradition. If they believe in a punitive God, I'm tempted to say, "Where did you get a God like this?"

> With someone of another faith we can start from a place of deep respect. I can be in a place of freedom where I won't judge or be judged by my own theology. When we get to a deep place of spiritual desire, matters of whose tradition is whose and where it comes from seem to matter very little.

Drawing on an image from Native American spirituality, Mary Ann Woodman asks her potential seekers to sketch a medicine wheel depicting the sources from which they draw wisdom in spiritual discernment processes. This spiritual practice helps Mary Ann to establish whether a spiritual direction relationship seems right. If it does, she enters into spiritual direction with a seeker utilizing their language and processes to facilitate spiritual growth.

Perhaps from the guide's standpoint the most vital aspect of guiding seekers from other traditions is the ability to witness how the One can move the souls of vastly different people from varied cultures and faiths in such diverse and yet ultimately similar ways:

> It fills me with wonder at how many ways the Divine expresses itself in human form and the creativity of the Spirit in finding ways to reach the human heart. Each of us has a path (or paths) that fits our culture, personality and vocation best but there comes a point where we can embrace that diversity within the Unity that is God.

6

WHERE SHALL THE SEEKER SEARCH?

All right, you say, I've now read about the nature of spiritual direction and its possibilities, benefits, and potential drawbacks. You've piqued my interest, but how do I begin? Where do I find a guide?

One answer is, "God will provide." Sharafuddin Maneri, the fourteenth-century Sufi sheikh and guide, put it this way, "Where will a novice find a sheikh? By what means can he recognize him as being the man? . . . Each one of those who seek God has been allotted all that is necessary for him."[1]

While Sharafuddin's answer might sound simplistic and even naïve, it does point to that aspect of grace that attends all truly meaningful guidance relationships. When guide and seeker are well suited in a way that cannot be contrived, it certainly appears to be, in part, a gift from above. Both seeker and guide sense that the spirit is at work in ways that transcend their individual and joint efforts.

A famous adage indicates that "When the student is ready the teacher will appear." And while this is true, another piece of folk wisdom reminds us that God helps those who help themselves. Therefore, the sections that follow are intended to help us help ourselves as we embark on the search for spiritual direction.

WHAT DO YOU SEEK?

In Chapter 3 we tried to distinguish the different types of counsel available to those wishing to explore spirituality and their inner lives. It is important for seekers to think carefully, to meditate and even pray for clarity in determining exactly what is needed at a particular moment in their journey. Do they have either immediate or long-standing problems they wish to resolve? Do they want to better understand the beliefs and practices of a certain faith or what that faith has to say about a specific issue that now confronts them? Are they ready to deepen their personal relationship with God and open to the possibility of change that such exploration might bring?

It might be helpful to again consider the different types of instruction and counsel available and the needs that might recommend one over another at certain points in one's life.

- If you are interested in learning about the beliefs, observances, and texts of a religion because you want to know more or seek to more fully identify with that faith community, you are seeking *religious education* or *formation*.

- If you want to relieve your anxieties and learn how to understand and deal with their causes, your are seeking *psychotherapy*.
- If you want insight into how the wisdom of a religious tradition might help you understand and respond to your problems, you are seeking *pastoral counseling*.
- If you wish to deepen your relationship with God so that you can recognize how God's spirit might be calling you and moving in your life, you are seeking *spiritual guidance*.

Please note that these various forms of learning and counsel are not mutually exclusive. It is not unusual at all for a person to be involved in two or more of them simultaneously. Many people of faith study in continuing religious education classes and seek out their clergy for pastoral counseling when the need arises. Similarly, any number of seekers participating in spiritual direction also see therapists on a regular basis. They desire to understand and relieve their problems while at the same time they wish to discover if there is transcendent meaning and a direction toward which their experiences are pointing.

The caveat is not to expect any of these forms of counsel and edification to do that which they are not intended to do. Ibn 'Abbad, the fourteenth-century Moroccan teacher of Islam, guarded against the mistake of confusing various kinds of counsel by making a distinction between two types of sheikhs. For basic religious formation and schooling in the requirements of Islamic law and the Sufi path, a novice would seek lessons from one or more "instructing" sheikhs. But if the seeker was ready for the kind of spiritual direction that is taught by exam-

nal association, Ibn 'Abbad would have him enter into a guidance relationship with an "educating" sheikh.[2]

When deciding whether spiritual direction is right for you at this moment in your life you might consider:

- Am I really sensing a lack of spiritual meaning in my life at this time, or is it something else that is missing?
- Do I have unresolved psychological issues that I need to address separately with a therapist, either before I enter into spiritual direction or concurrent with my being in guidance?
- If my life seems turbulent and chaotic, will spiritual direction be the most helpful for me at this time or might pastoral counseling offer a more fitting way to help me face present concerns in a religious context?
- Do I need additional religious instruction to help me better understand the beliefs, practices, and sacred texts that will all shape the underlying basis of my guide's counsel? If I have been raised in another faith and particularly another culture, do I first need to study and acquaint myself with my prospective guide's traditions to see if I feel comfortable enough with them to proceed?

In an age when people seek instant cures and technological fixes to eliminate their woes, it is important to remember that even the best spiritual guides wield no magic wands. Spiritual guidance can, in some ways, actually compound your problems.

> How do I express this opening to God, to live in the world and still love God? How much time should I spend in contemplation? With my partner? At my job? Serving the community? I'm just learning how to deal with these things.
>
> My partner, supportive and filled with goodness, still feels bemused and skeptical. We're not in the same place and this is not something we can share. The problem is I need to find balance. Actually, I find that trying to preserve my partner's comfort level is in itself a spiritual discipline.
>
> Where's it all going? I wish I knew.

As the preceding vignette shows, after a long and serious process directed by your guide, you may feel called to a path that could well overturn your life. Therefore, careful consideration must be made as to whether you are ready for the challenges spiritual direction might bring.

WHAT FORM OF GUIDANCE DO YOU NEED?

Most of our discussions so far have been based on the model of individual spiritual direction. While the details might vary between traditions, the overall premise remains pretty much the same—one guide and one seeker meeting with regularity to focus on discerning and deepening the unfolding relationship between the seeker and the Divine. There are, however, other forms of spiritual guidance that are worthy of consideration.

One of these is spiritual friendship or companionship. This kind of relationship very much resembles the model presented by Cicero in his dialogue *On Friendship*. Each of the two spiritual companions acts as guide for the other, listening, prayerfully and attentively, to his friend while offering insight as to how the spirit might be moving in his companion's life.

Spiritual friendship provided an important aspect of guidance in the Orthodox Jewish Musar movement. According to a Talmudic adage, "Make for yourself a master, but acquire for yourself a friend."[3] Thus spiritual companions were both to listen and to spur each other on to greater heights of learning and piety. A variation of this practice continues in the pairing of yeshivah students into study dyads, known as *chevrutas*.

For some, spiritual friendship can provide a moving, supportive, and highly personal form of guidance. However, such a relationship can be very hard to maintain. On a practical level, it is not easy for one companion to pour her heart out and then shift gears completely and listen with the openness and dispassion that her friend needs and deserves. The risk of too much emphasis and time being devoted to the spiritual searching of one of the partners is always present. In addition, factors that could affect the mutuality of guidance and impact upon the companions' relationship might include jealousy over a promotion, change of locale, or even a dispute between one of the companions and a third person who is close to both. It is for these reasons and others that companionship is probably the least practical form of spiritual guidance.

More prevalent is group spiritual direction. In a very real way, whenever people come together for worship, religious study or observance, reflection on sacred texts, or to hear a sermon or instruction, a form of group spiritual guidance is taking place.

Some Muslims gather in groups to chant the names and qualities of God. Mary, a retired psychiatric nurse who identifies with the Naqshbandi Order of Sufism, meets regularly with others on Chicago's South Side to join in this practice known as *dhikr*. Even though no formal discussion of personal religious issues occurs before or after the chanting, Mary feels that this group's practice helps sharpen her spiritual focus. "During the *dhikr* I let all distractions go. Everything that keeps me from thinking of God's oneness gets pushed away. It keeps me on track spiritually."

In the Buddhist tradition guidance may occur when people simply gather for silent, sitting meditation. In some instances there might be discussion before or after, and sometimes not. But those involved find their meditation and insights have been strengthened by the shared energy of others joining with them simultaneously on an inner journey.

A more formalized type of group direction occurs when a small number of people gather on a regular basis for guidance under the clear leadership of a group director. The focus of the group is not on helping its members solve their daily problems. Its intent is quite similar to that of individual spiritual direction, helping those in the group sense a greater openness to and recognition of God at work in their lives. This form of guidance draws on the example of the Apostles, the work of the seventeenth-century Jesuits, and of Methodism's founder, John Wesley, who in the eighteenth century brought Christians together in small groups for spiritual support and accountability. In this century such experiences were found in the permanent Group Reunion meetings held as weekly follow-ups for those who participated in the Cursillo Movement, a form of three-day retreat begun in Spain in 1949.[4]

Before the group meetings begin, a process of selection occurs whereby prospective participants confer with the leader to distinguish between the goals of group spiritual direction and group therapy, and to help determine whether the direction group is really for them. Sister Rose Mary Dougherty of Shalem, the moving force behind group spiritual direction today, suggests that groups begin with a half-day session to lay a foundation through prayer, shared reflection, and periods of silence. The group then sets the time and ground rules for subsequent meetings. Often these are monthly and last from one and a half to three hours. Group members commit themselves to regular attendance, respect for others in the group, confidentiality, and a willingness to share their spiritual journeys with each other.[5] Many groups agree to meet for a set number of months and then take a hiatus to allow members to decide if they wish to continue.

During the meetings prayer, silence, the sharing of one's experiences, and respectful responses from the group take place. The group leader is charged with facilitating the process and ensuring the emotional safety of the discussion. Of primary importance is maintaining the focus on God's presence in the life of the group and its members and gently restraining those who would monopolize the time or try to "fix" another's problems. The leader might also introduce the group to different forms of spiritual practice to try during and between sessions and to encourage members to keep a journal of their experiences.

For those who want to sample a variety of spiritual practices, group spiritual direction might be best. The response offered by the group provides a collective wisdom for each of its members. As each hears how God seems to be present for the others, he can become aware of God's presence in his own life and in the life of the group. Unlike individual spiritual direction, group direction affords the possibility of many faces of truth being uncovered in any given situation.[6]

Deborah Ann describes her experiences with group spiritual direction in this way:

> In group spiritual direction, I hear my questions, my fears, my joys, my yearnings, my confusion in the stories of everyone in the group, no matter who they are. . . . When I [first] thought about participating in a spiritual direction group I realized I wasn't comfortable in a group of Christians. I expected them to convert me. . . . I wondered if my being a Jew made them feel uncomfortable too. I'll never forget the relief I felt sitting in my first meeting and hearing someone who was Catholic say she was afraid *she* was committing heresy by being in the group.
>
> Negative experiences have been more in frustration over understanding the process, with people . . . responding by trying to "fix" someone else's problems on a psychological level. . . . I've seen others feel like they "weren't doing it right" or not being very comfortable with the unstructured nature of sharing. . . . [However] group spiritual direction broadens my perspective on spirituality, what constitutes a "spiritual" response or experiences, how different backgrounds and language influence how we process our spiritual experiences.

When deciding what type of spiritual guidance is right, a seeker might consider the following issues. While individual spiritual direction allows for deeper, freer, and more immediate communications with a director, it also presents the risk of dependency and the director exerting an undue influence on the seeker. For those who feel more comfortable relating in groups than in a one-on-one situation, group spiritual direction can offer richness through diversity, as the group members are affected by each other's experiences and insights. However, the possibilities for individuals to "hide" emotionally in the group is greater, as is the threat to confidentiality.[7]

WHERE TO LOOK

Once you have decided on what form you wish your spiritual direction to take, the next question is, Where do I find a guide? The first place you might look is your local church, synagogue, mosque, temple, or ashram. Call up and speak to a clergyperson or someone else in authority. Tell them exactly what it is you desire and perhaps set up a meeting. Because spiritual direction requires both time and special gifts, you might not find the right guide at first. However, your clergyperson might be able to help you clarify issues and point you toward someone who possibly could be a fitting director.

If you are on the margins of or are disaffected from your own faith community, you might look toward groups outside your tradition's mainstream who can respect your institutional difficulties while allowing you to touch the values of your own religion. Campus ministries, hospital or other institutional chaplaincies, monasteries, various renewal movements, and retreat centers might all be good places to contact. Many can be found in your phone book. Rather than eschewing all possibilities for guidance within your faith, you actually might find a bridge back to your own tradition.

Such was definitely the case for Stephen from Chapter 2. While working at the Follow Your Heart health-food market in the fall of 1982, he picked up a magazine called *New Age Source*. There on the front page was an article entitled "The High Holy Days as Meditation."

> At first I laughed, wondering if this was a joke or a satire. As I read on, I was taken by a story of the Baal Shem Tov, who taught that prayer could be meditation and worship transformational.

Rabbi Ted Falcon of the Los Angeles meditation synagogue, Makom Or Shalom, had written the article, so I went there for the holidays. It had been eleven years since I had entered a temple. I wound up standing in the back, the only one wearing a suit. Ted sat on a stool, speaking quietly, leaving space for our own intentions or to move about when we needed to. As we sang a wordless melody called a *niggun,* I was deeply touched. Slowly we began to chant words remembered from long ago, *Hineh Mah Tov.* . . . "How good it is for brothers and sisters to abide together." My heart opened and I cried like a baby. I finally felt at home.

Twice a month Makom Or Shalom offered meditation and scriptural study. Stephen became a regular and entered into spiritual direction with Rabbi Falcon, whom he still considers his guide. Inspired by his experiences, Stephen began a process of more formal Jewish study that ultimately led him to enroll in seminary. Today, as an ordained rabbi and chaplain Stephen offers counsel and spiritual guidance to other seekers along the way.

For those desiring additional resources from which to cull spiritual guidance please check the resources section beginning on page 179. There you will find a directory of various institutions representing different traditions that might prove helpful in your search, particularly if you want a guide from another faith.

WHAT TO LOOK FOR

A variety of factors should be considered when deciding if a particular guide is right for you. First and foremost is the question of the guide's own spiritual journey. Initially I prepared two questionnaires to gather information for this book from those who have participated in interfaith spiritual direction—one for seekers and one for guides. As the responses came back I quickly realized that the answers of the two groups varied in experience but not in kind. All of the guides were themselves active seekers. They differed from those they counseled only in that they had been journeying longer on the path. Eastern and Western traditions, no matter what name they call them, regard guides as those who have traveled along the spiritual road and are now helping others on the way. Since one cannot give to another that which he or she doesn't have, it is important that your guide continue to have an active prayer life (as he or she deems appropriate) and that he or she continues personally in some form of guidance relationship or peer review.

A talmudic passage says that the only sin that God really can't abide in this world is the sin of arrogance. When such pride occurs there is simply not enough room for both the prideful person and God. If this insight is true in general, it is certainly true when it comes to assessing the suitability of a spiritual director. Ultimately, guidance comes from God, and the director is only an instrument to help facilitate that process for the seeker. The guidance relationship should always remain focused on the movement of the spirit in the seeker's life, not on the guide or what the guide might be accomplishing.

While a certain sense of self-assurance and confidence is important, humility and wonder in the worship of God are key. There have been several times during my own guidance sessions when a striking realization has come to light. Whenever I thank my director, Sister Barbara Whittemore, her response is always the same: "Howard, this doesn't come from me. I'm just as surprised as you are. This comes from God, so let us give praise."

Questions of respective spiritual paths and faith traditions are important when evaluating any potential seeker/guide relationship. They take on added weight in an interfaith context. As we have seen in previous chapters, many who seek interfaith spiritual direction do so because they are looking for an aspect of spirituality that is not emphasized in their own tradition. Or they are drawn to the beliefs and practices of another faith, feeling that these better reflect their own experiences. Or they are looking for a more open, less directive approach to the Divine, to "pursue my agenda, not my religion's agenda for me." Regardless of which factors motivate the seeker, it is important that the guide have some understanding and respect for the seeker's own tradition.

The purpose of spiritual direction is to help the seeker grow and explore unexamined spiritual terrain. However, it is important for the guide to honor the seeker's underlying assumptions and beliefs and to know where the seeker is coming from. Being aware of differences in religious language and culture can help the guide and seeker bridge gaps and identify when the practice and concepts of their respective traditions are the same, analogous, or divergent.

Other factors to consider when searching for a director include:

- *Age.* Spiritual maturity occurs within different people at different times. However, the life experience and even the brokenness that comes to most of us only with middle age offers a greater possibility to distinguish the illusory from that which is of real value. Traditionally one could delve into kabbalah, the Jewish mystical journey, only after the age of forty, when one was both grounded and stripped of any false sense of immortality or self-sufficiency. Therefore you might wish to choose a guide who has come to the second half of life, with its awareness of human limitations and the resulting empathy that can come from such an awareness.

- *Experience.* If you are entering spiritual direction for the first time, you might feel somewhat unsure and vulnerable. A more seasoned director who is sensitive to your initial insecurities can help ease the transition as you begin to examine your life from God's perspective. As you grow in spiritual experience you will be better able to judge for yourself what is valuable, and you might choose a director of different style or tenor. During times of crisis and inner turmoil it is important to have an intuitive, empathic guide who can help you discern those experiences that seem to defy even your own description. Patience, prayerful support, and the guide's sympathetic perceptiveness are crucial so that you are not misled at such important and challenging times.

- *Gender.* If you have a choice between equally suitable guides you might want to choose one of the opposite gender. Both classical thought and contemporary psychology maintain that each of our psyches has a masculine and a feminine side. Gender complementarity in the guidance relationship might help you to uncover a suppressed part of your being that can further enrich your life and your relationship with God.

Two caveats: Because sexual attraction can be quite powerful, particularly in one-on-one relationships, care should be taken to minimize the possibility of crossing such boundaries. Especially those people with strong libidos might be wise to seek direction from guides of the gender and age that are least attractive to them. Also, if one has unresolved emotional issues with significant others of the opposite gender, it might be too difficult to develop an open, receptive guidance relationship with someone of that gender.

- *Personality Type*. Just as complementarity in gender might be a consideration in selecting a director, so might complementarity of personality style. We all are blessed with physical bodily instincts, emotions, and thoughts. However, different personality types seem to emphasize one of these functions over the other two. Therefore if you usually lead with your emotions, you might want a more reflective or instinctual guide. Conversely, if you tend to analyze everything dispassionately, you might seek a director who can help you come down from your head and become more in tune with your heart and body.

While all of the factors discussed above can help in determining whether a given spiritual direction relationship is right for you, there is still a large element of grace involved. A guide might meet all of your criteria in the areas of personal journey, experience, spiritual orientation, age, gender, and personality type, and yet, for whatever reason, you might just seem to get on each other's nerves. Or a guide might have few of the qualities you thought you were seeking, but there is something so right about the way the two of you interact that the other issues become unimportant.

As Sharafuddin noted: "When a . . . novice perceives in his own heart beauty in a sheikh he . . . draws peace and contentment . . . and can begin his [spiritual] search."[8]

THE COVENANT PROCESS

As you search for a spiritual guide keep in mind that you don't have to select the first person you meet. Sometimes the process of finding an appropriate director is not easy. If your search is not yielding results quickly, don't despair. Maintaining hope that God will provide as you continue your quest is, in itself, an important spiritual task.

Your initial interview with a prospective director will be a time of mutual examination. You will want to share your perceptions on the nature or function of spiritual guidance and see if your personalities mesh. It is crucial that you state exactly what it is you want, particularly if you are seeking direction from a guide of another tradition. As important as your sense of whether you can open your heart to this guide is your sense of whether the guide will respect your boundaries and not overtly or subtly influence you in a direction you feel the spirit is not leading you.

After some reflection and prayer you might mutually decide to give the relationship a try. Both of my spiritual directors suggested we begin with three meetings, one per month, and then evaluate our association. This gave us an opportunity to assess our rapport and to see if we were each being called to continue the relationship.

If you and your guide choose to continue, then you need to agree on the following:

- *Frequency of sessions.* Will you meet monthly? More often?
- *Agenda.* What should transpire during the sessions? Do you wish to begin or end with a prayer? Allow time for silent reflection? Do you wish your guide to function primarily as a mentor? A companion? One who supports you? One who challenges you? An advisor? A listening ear? What issues shall you discuss and how shall you avoid tangents and maintain the focus on God's movement in your life?
- *Between sessions.* In addition to holding each other in prayer, what should transpire from one meeting to the next? Agreed-upon spiritual tasks could include keeping a journal, reflecting on specific scriptural passages, trying new forms of private prayer and contemplative practice, silent retreat, and joining with a faith community for worship and charitable deeds.

The direction relationship establishes a certain accountability. Books and tapes are fine but they cannot replace the human factor. You will be more likely to carry out agreed-upon spiritual tasks knowing that there is another who cares about your growth than you might be if you were experimenting on your own.

You can also evaluate with your director whether these practices are enhancing or inhibiting your walk with God.

DISCERNMENT IN SPIRITUAL DIRECTION

As the process of guidance continues, by what means shall you evaluate the experience? On an interpersonal level, it will be important to assess your relationship with your guide on a regular basis, be it annually, semi-annually, or quarterly. This will afford both of you the chance to share your opinions on the positive aspects of your interactions and on what may be deterring or blocking your progress in your relationship with God. It might be time to change certain aspects of your arrangement or to end the relationship because it no longer seems viable or because you just wish to undertake the next part of your spiritual journey on your own.

Kerry Olitzky and Carol Ochs offer the following warnings to be considered as a regular part of the evaluation of your guidance relationship:

> If you feel unsafe or uneasy; if the discussion wanders into areas outside your agenda or you sense that the guide is leading you; if the guide or the process makes you feel bad, guilty or inadequate; and, most important, if you ever even begin viewing the guide as master, expert or guru—you are far better off with no spiritual guide but your own instincts.[9]

If you are involved in an interfaith guidance relationship there are some additional factors to consider. If the gap in culture or religious language is hindering real communication and progress, then you might wish to reconsider whether this is the right situation for you. This is doubly true if you feel that your guide is somehow urging you in a direction that you feel might violate your religious integrity. Some seekers have asked advice from their home clergy before entering into an individual or group interfaith guidance relationship. If you wish to keep contact with your own tradition it would be worthwhile to meet periodically with a clergyperson from your own faith. These meetings can provide you with another opportunity to assess your guidance relationship. You can learn if your tradition has concepts and practices analogous to those you've been reviewing with your director and, if not, why your faith advocates a different path. The clergyperson with whom you meet should generally be supportive of your spiritual path but also able to offer critique and a different perspective when needed.

On a personal level, you can evaluate the efficacy of your spiritual guidance by the changes that occur in your behavior and attitudes. In our society of fast foods and instant gratification you might be tempted to look for rapid transformation in your spiritual life. Don't! It takes time to "grow soul." The movement of the spirit can be very subtle, and increased spiritual awareness dawns slowly, requiring patience. However, when you find yourself no longer automatically angry or cynical in situations that used to elicit such responses, you begin to realize that something greater than yourself is working within you. When I now respond with more care and forbearance to bar and bat mitzvah students who come to lessons surly or unprepared, I still sometimes pause and ask myself, "Was that really me? What's happened?"

You might find yourself facing new circumstances, challenges, or insights and wonder what God might have you do instead of looking first for the logical or expedient answer. You can feel moved to look at scripture or your chosen tradition's precepts to help formulate your response. You might take the question into prayer or meditation and allow the voice of God to break through into your conscious mind. However, as Reverend George Aschenbrenner, director of the Jesuit Center for Spiritual Growth near Reading, Pennsylvania, reminds us, "Just because you have a thought, it doesn't mean that that is God."[10] Different traditions have various means of discerning whether our "personal revelation" experiences are ultimately transcendent or are self-aggrandizing in nature. It is well worth it to review both these methodologies and your new spiritual insights with your director.[11]

Perhaps the best evaluation of your guidance comes in two ways. The first is in your growing natural desire to invite God into your life, to live for something bigger and to look for the providential that underlies the seeming coincidences of existence. The second is when, with loving words and kind, charitable deeds, you allow God to act through you for the benefit of others. This desire is not motivated by any wish to exercise undue authority or impersonate God. Rather, it springs from the hope that you can be one of God's agents to bring a measure of healing to our broken world.

Part Three

THE SHAPE OF THINGS TO COME

CONTEMPORARY SPIRITUAL TRENDS

THE MODERN SYNTHESIS

As we begin the twenty-first century we might ask, What will the contours of our religious landscape be in the years ahead? Of course, anyone who tries to predict what is to come proceeds at great peril. A talmudic dictum indicates that normative prophecy ceased in Israel with the death of the last prophet, Malachi, during the fifth century BCE.[1] Since then, an adage contends, foretelling the future has become the province of little children and fools. Therefore, at the risk of seeming childish and foolish, let's try to distinguish some continuing spiritual trends and then try to understand where they might be heading.

In 1995 Tony Schwartz published a revealing book entitled *What Really Matters: Searching for Wisdom in*

America.[2] In it he describes his spiritual search that led him throughout America. He came in contact with varied types of philosophies, practices, and teachers. Yoga, psychology, dream work, and personality typing represent but a few of the movements he encountered during his quest.

As I read his account, one fact repeated itself again and again. Each of the teachers discussed in the book was born into one faith tradition and then was greatly influenced by others. Jack Kornfield, Joseph Goldstein, and Ram Dass (formerly known as Richard Alpert), all among the leading teachers of Eastern meditative practice in the United States, were all born into Jewish families. Michael Murphy, a pioneer of the human potential movement and founder of California's Esalen Institute, regularly attended an Episcopal church as a teenager with his grandmother. At Stanford University he delved into Eastern philosophies and then spent sixteen months at the ashram of the late Sri Aurobindo in Pondicherry, India, then under the leadership of "the Mother," Madame Richard. Helen Palmer, with whom I studied the Enneagram system of personality type, was baptized a Roman Catholic, has studied Aikido as well as Tibetan and Zen Buddhism, and is now finding a bridge back to Catholicism through her investigations of esoteric Christianity!

The views of nearly all the teachers cited by Schwartz have been profoundly influenced by the findings of various schools of modern psychology. Perhaps more telling is the fact that they all were born into Western faiths and have taken significant, if not primary, inspiration from different Eastern traditions. This reality does represent a trend among certain segments of our society.

When researching this book I had no problem finding Western seekers and guides who had been influenced by Eastern teachings and teachers. On the other hand, with the exception of Radha (Chapter 4) and some of Mary Ann's and Dale's seekers (Chapter 5), it was virtually impossible to locate seekers from Asian traditions who have taken spiritual direction with Western guides. My discussions with campus and military chaplains revealed that Indian and Asian seekers from other denominations did come for guidance, but all are affiliated with some form of Christianity. Perhaps this reflects the outcome of past Christian missionary work and the pressure Asian immigrants of other traditions feel to Americanize by embracing Christianity. Maybe the West has its own allure for those from the East.

A number of factors probably account for the fascination of Western seekers with Eastern traditions. Some we discussed in Chapter 2: the rise of telecommunications and the information age, population mobility and rapid world travel facilitating our interaction with other cultures here and abroad, and the breakdown of group identity and authority that allows us greater freedom to sample wisdom and customs from beyond home. More specifically, the meditative, introspective, and even renunciatory practices of some Eastern traditions offer a striking alternative to the pragmatic, other-directed, and acquisitive mores of Western society that are often mirrored in our American religious institutions. In addition, the exotic is alluring and the cultural differences and powers of intuition, breathing, and body control manifested by some Asian teachers give them a compelling, otherworldly aura. Of course, disillusionment can set in when it is found that these individuals can also have human foibles. Perhaps the most publicized of such reactions occurred in the 1960s when the Beatles discovered that their guru, the Maharishi Mahesh Yogi, despite contrary claims, had sexual desires like the rest of us.

As a result of his search, Schwartz speaks of:

> . . . an emerging American wisdom tradition that . . . emphasize[s] a comprehensive, balanced and integrated path to a complete life practice that addresses the body, mind and heart as well as the spirit . . . These integrated practices are a source of hope and promise. The flowering of more comprehensive approaches to wisdom, uniting the best of the East and the West, represents a historic first. . . . It's not just that there is wisdom to be found in America, but that these comprehensive approaches are emerging primarily in America.

Others sense this new synthesis that Tony Schwartz detects at the level of teaching and practice to be occurring on a more widespread popular level. Sister Rose Mary Dougherty, who participates in a Zen sitting meditation group that has recently moved its weekly meeting to her ecumenical Christian Shalem Institute, sees "a deep unity beginning to occur at the grassroots level. In a real sense we are coming together as human beings."[3]

Dr. Hillevi Ruumet, the psychologist and guide from Chapter 4, claims that it does matter that teachings and practices fit with who we are psychologically and culturally. She sees the major faith traditions as different paths to the same source that converge the farther we go, until they finally merge in the Great Mystery. To her, what matters is not the tradition as such, but the seriousness of those who seek and practice.

One respondent actually speaks of the loosening of our group boundaries and institutional authority as the work of providence leading us toward a greater spiritual integration of humanity: "God is a god who keeps on prying our hands loose from the petty stuff we hold on to so we can grasp what is really important. . . . Is the current dynamic of spirituality part of our general restlessness that moves us to switch jobs every five to six years? Or maybe God is simply bigger than any one church."

HISTORICAL ANTECEDENTS

It is true that people and traditions are coming together in today's America on a scale previously unknown. However, the interaction of philosophies and concepts in a way that sparks vital new approaches to wisdom and practice is not without precedent. The exchanges among Muslim, Christian, and Jewish philosophies during medieval times impacted all three faiths. Aristotelian philosophy, mediated through the writings of Islamic thinkers like Al-Farabi (d. 950), Avicenna (d. 1037), and later, Averroes (d. 1198), had a profound impact on Jewish philosophers like the Great Eagle, Moses Maimonides (d. 1204), and in turn, on seminal Christian thinkers including Saint Thomas Aquinas (d. 1274).[4] The works of these individuals literally transformed wisdom in the Middle Ages by reinterpreting the Bible, the rationale for God's existence, and the observance of religious law on the basis of rationalist philosophical principles.

The East has also known such cross-fertilization of traditions. These interactions have spurred further growth, sometimes through synthesis and sometimes by traditions having to reformulate their own doctrines to defend themselves intellectually through the writing of apologia. An example of both dynamics is found in this excerpt from a Chinese Buddhist defense of faith, *The Disposition of Error,* which appeared sometime between the fifth and sixth centuries CE.

The questioner said: Confucius stated, "The barbarians with a ruler are not so good as the Chinese without one." Mencius said, "I have heard of using what is Chinese to change what is barbarian, but I have never heard of using what is barbarian to change what is Chinese. You sir, at the age of twenty learned the way of Yao, Shun, Confucius, and the Duke of Chou. But now you have rejected them, and instead have taken up the arts of the barbarians. Is this not a great error?

Mou Tzu said: What Confucius said was meant to rectify the way of the world, and what Mencius said was meant to deplore one-sidedness. Of old, when Confucius was thinking of taking residence among the nine barbarian nations, he said, "If a gentleman-scholar dwells in their midst, what baseness can there be among them?" The Commentary says, "The north polar star is in the center of heaven and to north of man." From this one can see that the land of China is not necessarily situated under the center of heaven. According to the Buddhist scriptures, above, below and all around, all beings containing blood belong to the Buddha-clan. Therefore I revere and study these scriptures. Why should I reject the Way of Yao, Shun, Confucius, and the Duke of Chou? Gold and jade do not harm each other; crystal and amber do not cheapen each other. You say that another is in error when it is you yourself who does err.[5]

There is even a view that, more than a faith, Christianity itself represents an integrated approach that synthesized aspects from any number of ancient wisdom traditions. These include the ethics of ancient Israel, the philosophy of Greece, the organization and sense of loyalty to doctrine found in Rome, and the transformation of personal redemption prevalent in Near Eastern mystery cults.[6]

Christianity's ability to refashion and incorporate these various elements might help account for its religious and political predominance over other traditions as the West moved from antiquity to the Middle Ages.

COUNTERVAILING TRENDS

One of the first laws of physics states that for every action there is an equal and opposite reaction. The same axiom can be applied to our religious and social scene. Just as there is a strong movement today toward universalism and cross-fertilization of traditions, so there is a strong, sometimes violent, movement to maintain particularity and to refortify boundaries. To verify this fact, all we have to do is recall the headlines of recent years highlighting the ongoing religious ethnic conflicts in the Balkans, India, and the Middle East.

In 1995, Benjamin Barber published a book with a most intriguing title: *Jihad vs. McWorld: How Globalism and Tribalism Are Reshaping the World*. The overall premise of the text is the modern dichotomy between two opposing forces—global consumer capitalism with its dissolving of social and economic barriers, and ethnic/religious divisions that can separate populations into ever-smaller tribe-like units. And lest we think that this struggle between universalism and particularism is solely economic and taking place only beyond our shores, Barber reminds us:

> To Americans, *jihad* [doing battle against perceived evil] is often taken to be a foreign phenomenon, a feature of Middle Eastern politics. But we can to-day also speak of an American *jihad* . . . of [those] who rebel against the 'culture of disbelief' . . . in their judgment . . . there is much . . . that is sickening, that outrages elementary justice and morals. . . . The yearning of [some] American suburbanites for

> the certainties of a literal New Testament are no
> less . . . than the yearning of Arabic martyrs for the
> certainties of a literal Koran.[7]

More moderate expressions of this yearning can be found in the Christian Coalition's efforts to reinstitute organized prayer and the teaching of creationism in public schools. It can also be found in nativist efforts to bar or restrict services to new immigrants. Its most extreme, terrifying face is revealed in the outrage of white supremacist militias and in actions like the 1995 Oklahoma City bombing.

On an intellectual level, evidence of this desire to circle the wagons can be found in the late 1990s attempt by the Catholic Church to ensure the doctrinal orthodoxy of those teaching at Catholic colleges. I also know of at least one instance at an Orthodox Jewish academy where a noted philosopher was pressured to retract some of his writings due to differences over matters of creed. Perhaps the most shocking incident of this kind that I observed first-hand occurred the time I participated in a faculty colloquium at a sectarian institution of higher learning. The discussion between the guest lecturer and those academics present was far-ranging and stimulating. When we concluded, the person recording the session asked how the tapes should be titled. My fellow respondents turned fearfully adamant, insisting there should be no date, name of place, or other attribution listed, lest their jobs be endangered. To this day I can't believe that such a scene occurred in these United States where freedom of speech and assembly are the law of the land.

Universalism and Particularism

At this point it would be tempting to draw a line in the sand. On the side of goodness and light we would place the forces impelling us toward relaxing our boundaries, synthesizing our wisdom traditions, and coming closer to one another. On the side of darkness and harm, we would locate all dynamics that reinforce limits, define differences in creed, and maintain group distinctions. And then, in good apocalyptic form, we could extrapolate trends that show the universal domain surging as the realm of particularism recedes. The ultimate goal: that which most messianic visions foresee—a united humanity joined in an unbroken communion of spirit with the Divine.

This picture of the future certainly sounds idyllic. It may even come to pass—but probably not until the dawning of some post-historic era of redemption, if at all. In real time it is probably as facile as it is wrong simply to place unity in the camp of the angels and particularity on the side of darkness. As we should realize, the dynamic between these two trends is far more complex. Phenomena that we thought would lead us in a unifying direction sometimes lead us in the other way—or in both directions at the same time. The information highway that is transforming our world into a global village can also atomize us into solitary individuals alone in our rooms, glued to our keyboards and monitors, without any real human interactions at all.

There is much to recommend universalism. However, when taken to the extreme, it can deny historically significant forms of human association, leaving us adrift without roots or a sense of ever being at home. It is hard to relate equally to all of humanity at once. The respondents in this book, all of whom draw guidance from various traditions, agree that one needs a place to start. That familiarity of culture and language is important when embarking on a spiritual quest. It can also reassert its importance further down the path.

Particularism does have its drawbacks. Some of them can be exclusionary, restrictive, and quite ugly. However, there is an appropriate place and an enduring power to the bonds of kinship, language, and common history. In what can be an undifferentiated sea of humanity, they give us a sense of social location and belonging. Rather than just flowing along, we can establish footholds in supportive communities that we can count on, and which in turn should be able to count on us. Charity given only at "home" is insufficient. But "home" does provide us with a socializing environment and a place to begin.

Kabbalah, the Jewish mystical tradition, envisions God's personality as being revealed through ten different manifestations, known as the *sefirot*. The most common configuration of these *sefirot* is the *Etz Chaim,* the Tree of Life, pictured below.

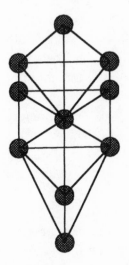

The right column of the tree, as you look at it, is the side of wholeness, the overflowing greatness of God's love. The left column represents the defining power of God's judgment that sets proper boundaries, categories, and limits. Only when both of these sides are in proper balance can the center column transmit the divine radiant energy from the higher realms to the lower ones in full measure and beauty.

If wholeness and particularity are both constituents of the Divine, then surely we must need to respect and manifest both dynamics in our quest for the Divine. Newly developing phenomena in interfaith spiritual direction might just help us achieve that sacred balance we need.

MEETING AN INTERFAITH SPIRITUAL GUIDE

Most of those offering inter-faith spiritual direction today come from one of two backgrounds. Some were born into the faith they now practice and have attracted seekers from a variety of traditions for reasons discussed in earlier chapters. Others converted to or formally adopted their current religion and offer counsel to others who are now exploring a similar spiritual path. It is rare to find a guide who by training and conscious choice is an interfaith spiritual director. Mary Ann Woodman and Dale Rhodes are two such guides. Another is Claude d'Estrée, who also helps train interfaith directors.

Claude d'Estrée was raised in the Russian Orthodox Church and, as an adult, actually served that church as a subdeacon. He received his formal education under Jesuit supervision at Catholic parochial schools. Yet from the time he was eleven he became interested in the teachings of Buddhism.

While attending the Harvard Divinity School he furthered his pursuit of both traditions. During the late 1970s he studied and then taught centering prayer with the Trappist monk M. Basil Pennington, then of Saint Joseph's Abbey in Spencer, Massachusetts. He also had the opportunity to meet the fourteenth Dalai Lama of Tibet during his first visit to the United States in 1979, and he has continued study under his guidance. Claude graduated from Harvard Divinity School in 1980 having written a thesis comparing Buddhist, Christian, and Jewish spiritual practices. In 1981 he was recognized by the Dalai Lama as a *löpon,* a master teacher of Buddhism, and was appointed the first Buddhist chaplain at Harvard.

Faculty appointments brought both Claude and his wife, Dr. Tamra Pearson d'Estrée, to the University of Arizona in 1990. There, at Tucson's Saint Philip's-in-the-Hills Episcopal Church, Claude and Dr. Jeanette Renouf founded Tacheria, a Multifaith Centre for Spirituality, Reconciliation, and the Sacred Arts. As Claude recalls, people from various backgrounds including church-going and unchurched Christians, Buddhists, and marginally practicing Jews, all came for spiritual guidance. Under the umbrella of Tacheria, Claude and Jeanette began to develop a two-year training program for multifaith guides, the New School for Spiritual Directors. Claude and Tamra now live in Fairfax, Virginia. Tamra teaches Conflict Resolution at George Mason University. Claude serves there as Buddhist Chaplain and is also a monk at a local Korean temple, the Temple of a Thousand Buddhas. He continues to teach centering prayer in the contemplative Christian tradition and does chronic pain and grief counseling.

I first met Claude on an April afternoon in 1999. Over lunch he began to share with me his experiences with interfaith spiritual direction.

HOWARD: Claude, I'm curious. What kind of people seek out an interfaith spiritual director?

CLAUDE: Actually, people come to me from a variety of backgrounds. Some hear of me by word of mouth. Others have taken one of my classes in Buddhism or meditation or world religions and sense that they can trust me. Interestingly enough, in Tucson a number of people suffering from chronic fatigue syndrome sought me out.

HOWARD: Given your own training in both Buddhism and Christianity, what models do you draw on in your work?

CLAUDE: The figure of the Russian *staretz*, particularly as modeled by Saint Seraphim, is very powerful for me. The *staretz* would try to read the seeker's heart, to discover the question behind the question being asked.

In Buddhist tradition a teacher, an elder, tries to "polish the mirror." Through his words and gestures he would reflect the seeker's own traits back to him. Hopefully, seeing yourself reflected that way would lead to greater self-examination and growth. However, when seekers come to me they wouldn't initially know that I'm Buddhist.

HOWARD: Why not?

CLAUDE: Because my goal is to train them to be their own spiritual directors, to set their own definitions so that I become a friend upon the journey.

HOWARD: So let's start at the beginning. Take me through what happens when a seeker first comes to you.

CLAUDE: Since I believe that each person's faith leads through his or her birth religion, we start with something called a faith background check. Every new seeker needs to compose their own spiritual autobiography. While most write essays, some have brought in paintings, poetry, graphs or their life's history arranged in bullet notes.

The next step is for them to check off the most important events—what really stands out for them. They need to offer their own reading of both the secular and what they consider the sacred aspects of those events. As we peel back the events, going deeper into them, certain terms begin to appear defining that person's relationship to the world and to the sacred.

HOWARD: Could you give me an example?

CLAUDE: Well . . . someone might be reflecting on something that happened to them, something really tragic, and say, "This really makes me wonder if God is just!" Then we'll begin to explore just what they mean by divine justice or the lack of it. Do they mean justice like the United States legal system, with trials and verdicts and punishments? Do they mean justice as in there might be some kind of ultimate balance in the world?

While the terms are theirs, I want them to be alert to the provisional nature of their definitions. As they grow and their spiritual life deepens, the meaning of these terms for them, including the term *God,* will change. Sometimes they'll even defy articulation and touch the ineffable.

HOWARD: You know, throughout this process there seems to be something missing. Shouldn't some scripture or spiritual practice play a role, even within your multifaith approach?

CLAUDE: Unless the seeker brings it up, I usually don't introduce scripture until we're further down the road. Then I'll give them an assignment to bring in something they remember from their religious past. Usually they come with Psalm 23, "The Lord is my shepherd . . ." or maybe the Lord's Prayer.

Sometimes they bring in a hymn or passage that pushed them out of their church, usually some liturgical leftover extolling that faith's hierarchy or its patriarchal view of women. They might become really vehement against their birth faith or against all belief. We have to explore that vehemence. I want to help them break their old paradigms, to deconstruct what came before. What seemed real in the prayer life of a five-year-old just no longer applies to a fifty-year-old. Even if they choose a Buddhist path, their anger at their birth religion will rot their Buddhism if it's left unresolved.

HOWARD: So how might you determine whether Buddhism or another approach is right for any given seeker?

CLAUDE: One thing I want to determine is if someone is really on a theistic or nontheistic path.

HOWARD: What do you mean?

CLAUDE: Simply put, theistic traditions like Hinduism, Judaism, Christianity, Islam believe that reality equals the universe plus one, the Divine. Nontheistic paths like Buddhism contend that the universe is all there is and that all beings, though impermanent, are interconnected.

If a seeker told me he or she had a vision where they felt themselves merging with a great light, I would ask them how they interpreted the experience. If they told me that they felt they had become something beyond what they had previously been, that might indicate a theistic stance. In our future meetings we would look at their life from the standpoint of where God's will might be leading them and how the spirit might be moving within their life.

On the other hand, they might interpret the experience of uniting with the light as a reflection of their deep interconnectedness with all beings. That answer might lead me to conclude that theirs was a truly nontheistic path. However, even then if they wished to explore Buddhism for themselves, I would first help them explore whether they couldn't find in their own faith what they felt they wanted from Buddhism.

HOWARD: But why? After all, you are a *dharma* teacher and an ordained Buddhist monk.

CLAUDE: Out of my own experience as a Western Buddhist I know that it can be lonely. There is not much of a community and it doesn't include your family and friends. Our shrines here reflect another culture, be it Tibetan, Thai, or Korean. However, if we go through the entire process and the seeker still wants to explore Buddhism then we go for it.

HOWARD: What do you think are some of the pluses and minuses of this interfaith approach?

CLAUDE: The thing that I worry about most is the lack of serious commitment to practice. Some people just want to pick and choose different elements from different faiths because they want to feel good. Others are looking for a guru to take over responsibility for their lives.

The fact is, I know of too many cases where people say they've survived spiritual direction because their guide had an agenda.

The Dalai Lama taught us, "The purpose of life is to develop the warm heart. If you can, help others. If you cannot do that, at least do them no harm." I always try to keep that in mind. What good is it to meditate for twenty-five years if you still act towards others like an S.O.B.? The truth is I can't work with everybody. If they want a guru relationship, that's not me. We can share the journey. I can be the guide, but neither I nor anyone else can move the rocks or cover the potholes of another's life.

As we finished the discussion and lunch, our waitress came over and sat down at our table. She told us her name was Mindy and asked if I was a rabbi because she'd noticed that I was wearing a yarmulke. After Claude and I introduced ourselves she began to tell us her story. She herself was Jewish, though she claimed it had been a while since she had last visited a synagogue. Her sister had become a Buddhist and recently had been married in a Buddhist ceremony in Boulder, Colorado. She recounted how her Jewish grandmother had gone out for the wedding. After Mindy got up, Claude and I both agreed that today's America really is a global village of faith. Here was a Conservative rabbi, in spiritual direction with a Catholic religious order, having lunch with a Buddhist *löpon* of Russian Orthodox descent. And, together with a young woman working as a server, we three had been holding our own impromptu world congress of religions.

THE GROUP

It was now July. Three months has elapsed since Claude and I shared a meal and our views on religion and spiritual direction. During a phone conversation he invited me to attend a meeting of his Buddhist sitting meditation group that was to occur that Thursday. Eager to share in the experience, I quickly accepted the invitation and took down the directions to Virginia. That Thursday, July 22, marked the second most important fast day in the Jewish calendar, the Ninth of Av, anniversary of the destruction of the First and Second Holy Temples in ancient Jerusalem. As soon as our afternoon services were completed, I jumped in my car, suitcase in hand, and headed for Virginia.

Several hours later I pulled up at our designated place of meeting, a Korean Buddhist temple near Fairfax. Claude had yet to arrive and, after a few less-than-successful attempts at communicating with the shrine's staff, I waited until he came. Upon his arrival, Claude took me into the sanctuary. My attention was immediately drawn to a huge golden statue of the Buddha, placed at the front of the room. Claude explained that the statue had actually been moved from its regular place because this coming Sunday a festival was to occur. Two new Buddha statues were to be dedicated—one to be placed on each side of the current statue. Lanterns and streamers adorned the ceilings, each representing a different family within the congregation.

As Claude showed me the different ritual objects, we came to a part of the sanctuary set off by a screen. Looking behind the partition I saw a small shrine with photographs and black vertical tablets. This area was a place of memorial, reflecting the Confucian element of ancestor veneration that has become part of Zen Buddhism in China, Korea, and Japan. As Claude described to me the different Buddhist mourning customs, it occurred to me that those black tablets played exactly the same role that our synagogue memorial plaques played.

This sense of functional equivalence became more pronounced as Claude directed my attention to the ceiling-high rows of shelves on the sanctuary's front wall. On these shelves were three small golden statues, each a Buddha whose hand gesture, or *mudra*, was slightly different. Claude explained that the goal was for those shelves to hold one thousand golden Buddha statues, thus fulfilling the vision articulated in the shrine's name. He also told me that each congregational family was expected to donate at least one statue as part of the Temple's major fundraising drive. Dedicatory items? Fundraising campaigns? Perhaps certain aspects of religious institutional life remain constant despite differences in language, culture, and belief.

As my tour concluded, two members of the meditation group arrived, Steven and Louis. Together we departed for a local park where the others would join us for that night's sitting. When we had all assembled Claude gave me the chance to speak with the group before meditation began. So that the group members might express themselves freely, he departed for a walk.

The backgrounds of those present were as different as the number of people there. Louis, a student at George Mason, was first exposed to Buddhism in a course on Asian religions he had taken at the University of Wurzberg in Germany. The grandson of a minister and the son of hippie parents, he described his religious upbringing as "vaguely Protestant." Steven's father is Jewish and his mother is Catholic. In an attempt to please both grandmothers he was baptized and bar-mitzvahed. A federal government worker, Steven was drawn to Buddhism's respect for all living things, reflecting his own sensitivity to animals.

Geoff and Terri are married to each other. Geoff grew up completely unchurched and only began to consider religion due to some interactions with Mormon friends. After reading a book on world religions he found Buddhism most compelling, particularly the compassionate teachings of the Dalai Lama and the Buddhist belief in reincarnation. Terri, who had been previously married to a devout Catholic, now considers herself an "evangelical Buddhist." She had initially resisted Geoff's invitations to join the group. But she had always wondered where our energy goes after death, and when, after a long illness she went back to school, she found herself in class with a Buddhist nun, she took it as a sign. She began attending meditation and now derives such great equanimity and personal benefit from the sessions that she regularly tries to recruit everyone she knows to join.

Marilyn grew up in a small southern town and still considers herself Jewish. Her interest in Buddhism began after the death of her infant son some years ago. Finding no solace or answers in the counsel of a rabbi she had called, at a friend's suggestion she read *The Tibetan Book of Living and Dying*. She finally took comfort in an idea she discovered there: Perhaps her son had been a unique, actualized soul, who only needed to come to earth for a short while to teach her a lesson about life, albeit a painful one. While still interested in exploring Jewish spirituality, she gains a sense of inner peace from her meditation.

Rounding out the group that night were two relative newcomers. Dave, a former colleague of Geoff, had only been coming for a short while. Adam, of Asian descent and Christian upbringing, was there for the first time, having seen the meeting publicized on the Internet.

As we sat around a picnic table, members of the group began to explain what takes place when they gather. Unlike the spiritual direction groups described in Chapter 6, the focus of these sessions is not on the members sharing their experiences with each other. Instead, their gathering consists of two parts. In the first part Claude might discuss some aspect of Buddhist thought. A favorite topic is the practice of mindfulness, how to be fully present to the possibilities and blessings of each moment. This can be accomplished be realizing that much of our anxiety comes not from what is happening at present but from preconceived ideas based on our past experience or on fears of what will occur in the future. A nervous lecturer might be consumed by memories of having been mocked following a prior speech, or by the anticipation of being criticized after delivering her next address. Serenity can be achieved by letting go of the past,

which is no longer real, and the futr
only aspects of our imagination. 154
then followed by different meditation c.
those present look inward and achieve the equ..
they seek.

As the discussion went around the table, those present described what it is they gain from these sessions.

> LOUIS: It's easier to meditate with a group. When we
> meditate there is a peaceful energy that surrounds
> us. I feel aware of physical changes going on within
> me until it is hard to find any division between my
> body and my mind. We need to meditate individual-
> ly, to make it on our own, but we need the group as
> well to call us back.

> TERRI: We smile and nod to each other. We don't al-
> ways know each other's names but we're joined in
> shared meaning. It helps me regroup for the next week.
> If I've had some trouble, being with the group reminds
> me of the practices I want to carry over into my life.

It was fascinating to hear how just being present in
the group helped the members to achieve greater spiritual
intentionality in their lives without explicitly discussing their
joys and sorrows. They are able to draw the insights and
support they need from Claude's talks and their meditation.

Equally fascinating was their discussion about
Buddhism and institutional religion.

> STEVE: Organized religion puts too much emphasis
> on fees.

> MARILYN: When it comes to the High Holy Days, you
> have to buy tickets to go to services. I know that syn-
> agogues only charge these fees once a year and don't
> pass the plate weekly. Still there's something that
> seems wrong about paying to pray.

GEOFF: You know guys, I've been to other Buddhist groups where they have lists of fees for different services and schedules of "suggested donations." Some start at forty dollars a session.

STEVE: You're kidding!

GEOFF: No, I'm not. And in some groups the emphasis seems to be less on the inner life and more on when you made your last trip to Nepal or which famous monk you know. You would have thought they were discussing rock stars.

All agreed that they were attracted to Claude's group because his approach was both intellectual and very much down to earth. They expressed real appreciation that his teachings and the insights they draw from his words and meditations have real applications in their daily lives.

TERRI: It has led me to much healthier living. When I feel distress or anger I can just let it go. I remember that what is, is. I breathe and it's over. I've found a great equanimity that I've never felt before.

MARILYN: I find myself trying to be more mindful even when I'm driving my car. When I get angry or sad I visualize my feelings to be leaves floating on a river. As they drift downstream I just let them go.

GEOFF: As head of my own company I feel completely different about being responsible for my employees and their families. I've learned to set limits, to put a cap on my anger. There's just so much I'm willing to get upset about and after that I've learned to step back and not hold on to these feelings.

STEVE: I've always had problems when I live in the future or in the past. Living in the present brings me back to where I need to be.

Just then Claude returned from his walk. Instead of joining us at the table, he went over to a blanket on a knoll several yards away. As he assumed the lotus position he brought us back to where we needed to be. Without uttering a word, he returned us to the need of the moment, which was letting go of our discussion and joining in the evening's meditation.

The practice that night was an openness meditation that began with an attempt to just be aware of the sensations we were experiencing at present. We then were called to follow the rising and falling of our breath while letting go of all distracting thoughts and feelings. As the exercise progressed we were asked to lie back and gaze at the vastness of the heavens, allowing any memories or plans or anxieties to just float upward and away. We concluded by sitting up once again and contemplating an aspect of the nature that surrounded us: a tree, a plant, a blade of grass. After sharing our reactions to the exercise we bid each other farewell and went our separate ways.

When I remember my experiences of that night I recall feeling a great sense of peace and tranquillity, feelings that are rare for me. I also remember thinking that aspects of that meditation were similar to certain practices found in Hasidism and kabbalah. Claude's instruction to let any distracting feelings or thoughts float up to the sky mirrors a teaching of Hasidism's founder, Rabbi Israel Baal Shem Tov. The Baal Shem Tov taught that when you experience a *machshavah zarah,* an alienating thought, you should allow that thought to ascend back to its origin, one of the manifestations of God's personality on the Tree of Life. Therefore, if you are feeling unduly critical, those thoughts should be allowed to rise until they reach their ultimate root, the divine attribute of Judgment, known in Hebrew as *Din.*

Additionally, when Claude told us to concentrate on our breathing patterns he guided us to note the pause between the moment we exhaled and the time we took our next breath. That pause is reminiscent of the emptiness that precedes all action, the emptiness in which everything is possible because nothing as of yet has been formed. This realization is similar to one advanced by the thirteenth-century kabbalist Rabbi Joseph Gikatilla. One of Gikatilla's spiritual practices was a breathing exercise based on the tetragrammaton, the ineffable four-letter name of God (YHWH). After exhaling, while envisioning the last H of the Divine name, the person meditating is asked to visualize the initial Y without breathing. That space represents the unbounded fullness of God's essence, known as *Ayn Sof* (Without End), before the transition is made to the revealed aspects of God's personality, the *sefirot* on the Tree of Life. It is only after noting the potential for everything to be found in the boundless God who is "no thing" that we inhale once again while imagining the Divine name's second letter, H.

READING THE HEART

During my night in Virginia I had the opportunity to ask some of the group about their experiences with Claude in one-on-one spiritual direction. They all indicated how they admired his ability to balance the experiential and the intellectual. They each felt that Claude's life experience gave them a sense of reassurance. If they were facing a challenge or crisis, Claude's guidance seemed very applicable to their lives because it seemed as if he'd faced a similar situation before.

One seeker said that he appreciated how Claude never gave you the answer, that he opened new spiritual vistas for you to consider and explore yourself. Another group member agreed saying, "When you ask a question, Claude will sometimes respond by asking whether you should really be considering a deeper question instead." I later discovered that this was what Claude meant by the guidance technique of "reading the heart," as exemplified to me later that night in the following account:

> I came to Claude sorely troubled because my fiancé and I were breaking up. Since I've always had problems with abandonment and rejection, who better to consult than a Buddhist guide? After all, Buddhism is all about living mindfully in the present, about letting go of those yearnings and memories and imaginings that are the root of our sorrows.
>
> As we sat down I told Claude my problem and asked if he could suggest some spiritual practice to help me let go of my sense of rejection. Instead he looked at me softly and inquired, "Who is it who feels rejected?" Good question. One that stopped me dead in my tracks. I thought a long time before I replied.
>
> "I guess it's the little girl who never felt she could please her parents. And maybe the woman who is wondering how others will react when they hear of the breakup."
>
> "Is the little girl here any longer?" Claude asked.
>
> "No, she's been gone for a long time," I answered.
>
> "That's right. And what do you fear about the reaction of others, if you and your fiancé break up?"
>
> Tears came to my eyes as the impact of this question washed over me. "I fear that it will prove what I've known all along, that I am essentially unlovable."
>
> With compassion, Claude asked me to look within once again. "Let go of the past, forget the future. As things are right now, is there anything about you that is unlovable?"
>
> I thought long and hard until I could finally utter the word "No."

Feeling quite drained and relieved, I thought our session was drawing to a close. Not quite. Claude glanced over and asked a final question. "What positive effect have you been drawing by holding on to this sense of being unlovable?"

"I don't know what you mean."

"I think you do," said Claude. "You've been holding on to this self-image as the rejected, unlovable child for a long time. You must get something positive out of it."

Silent seconds turned into long quiet minutes as I pondered the shattering importance of this challenge. When I spoke it was hard for me to even form the words.

"I guess that the sense of rejection and the need to overcome despair has been the fuel I've been running on for a long time. It's comfortable because it's what I know. Also I think I've been confusing pity with love, figuring that if people show me compassion, that will replace the unconditional acceptance I never received at home. If you wallow in your wounds it relieves you of some responsibility to meet expectations and do positive things to gain real affection."

Since that session with Claude, my spirit has been more joyous. No matter what happens with my fiancé I can now hear the positive things people say about me and try to retain that same joy. When I feel low I can pause and breathe and ask, "Who is it that's feeling rejected?" Just stopping and posing the question allows the anxiety to dissipate and a new sense of equanimity to take hold.

SPIRITUAL TOURISTS

When Claude and I first met over lunch he told me about a meeting of Christian Trappist monks and Buddhist monks that he had helped coordinate during the seventies. He remarked how this experience had led him to conclude that even if religions differed in dogma, culture, and organization, there was a real connection at the contemplative level. Thus the Dalai Lama and Thomas Merton could find no basic disagreement among themselves because they were able to speak to each other from the depth of their souls, celebrating both their commonality and the cultural differences.

I agreed with Claude that there seemed to be a commonality among faiths at the contemplative level. My own research had revealed that many of the practices used by spiritual guides carried over from one tradition to the next. Meditations based on following your breath or repeating a sacred verse, extended retreats, prayer cells, and the spiritual companioning of friends could all be found in two or more traditions, no matter by what names those practices are called.

However, I told Claude that after visiting the Temple of the Thousand Buddhas it seemed our different faiths shared more than just a few common meditative practices. Memorial plaques and fundraising campaigns complete with dedicated giving opportunities always seem to go on in every religious institution. He looked at me and smiled.

> You know, Howard, what happens at that Buddhist temple on Sunday is the same thing that happens in every church in this country. People come as families, they celebrate their traditions, they bond together and have disputes with one another—just like anyplace else.
>
> It is difficult for me even though I am a monk at the temple and can't see myself as anything but a *dharma* teacher. I don't speak Korean and often don't feel a part of what's going on. I only attend the temple every other Sunday because my family doesn't go with me. On the opposite weeks we take our son to a church in the area where he and Tamra feel a sense of connection to the service and community.

I told Claude that I had discussed this matter of cultural difference and institutional similarity with the group when I had spoken to them before the meditation. Most interesting had been the response of Louis, who simply said, "Don't you know what the appeal is? We're tourists. We visit the meditation aspect we like on a weekly basis and are able to leave out the rest."

Until long after midnight Claude and I discussed whether he or any of us involved in interfaith spiritual guidance are anything but tour guides. We show seekers the good neighborhoods while leaving the more boring or seamy stops off the itinerary. We questioned whether most seekers are looking for a good feeling without the willingness to undertake the ongoing disciplines of any faith necessary to lead a deeply spiritual and good life.

Claude laughed ruefully when he told me about certain Buddhist seekers who wear as many red protection threads around their necks as Mr. T used to wear gold chains. According to the Tibetan Buddhist tradition, when a seeker is initiated into a given spiritual practice, he or she receives a protection thread and blessing from the master who taught that practice. The object is to continue the practice regularly after you have taken the initiation. In Judaism we have a similar notion that once you begin observing a commandment you should continue. Most Buddhists usually have one main practice and maybe one or two others. Judging by the number of threads he has observed some seekers wearing, Claude knew they weren't carrying on every practice because if they were, they'd have no time to do anything else!

Lest despair take over, I told Claude of the difference his guidance had made in the lives of those in his group. He responded that even if they don't meditate daily, if they bring some sense of mindfulness with them and it conditions how they act and interact, maybe that is enough. I reminded Claude that most traditions use terms like *path, journey,* and *way* to describe the life of the spirit and that those who counsel others are often called companions or guides. We concurred that in this age of spiritual seeking and individual autonomy only a few will dedicate themselves completely to the injunctions and practices of any faith. Perhaps our best hope is that we can influence our "tourists of faith" so that even in between sessions they continue to regard the map seriously.

———————

——————————

THE MODERN SPIRITUAL PARADOX

UNIVERSAL OR PARTICULAR?
TO SEEK OR TO DWELL?
TOURIST OR RESIDENT?

These questions seem to mark the great religious paradox of today. For many of us the spirituality of settlement exemplified by *Pleasantville* in the fifties is no longer satisfying or even a viable choice. While it offered communal support and a sense of certainty, its demands for conformity left little room for the individual to explore different paths or to seek a personal relationship with God. Our current spirituality of seeking has opened new vistas of religious expression. However, it can also tempt seekers to play an "all-star game" of religion. Rather than seriously committing to any path, they might tend to pick and choose elements from different traditions based solely on whether these make them feel good.

Psalm 27, cited at the end of Chapter 2, expressed its author's desire to "dwell in the Lord's house . . . to gaze upon the splendor of the Lord and to visit within God's sanctuary." This prayer gave voice to a heartfelt desire—to be both a resident and a visitor in God's sanctuary at the same time. Rather than seeing these two types of spiritual expression as conflicting, a choice of either/or, the psalmist sensed that they might somehow be brought together in a "both/and" embrace.

In 1992 Barry Johnson published a book entitled *Polarity Management*[1] in which he explored the difference between a problem and a polarity. A problem is a difficulty that can be resolved with a certain finality. "Where shall we have lunch today?" is solved when we choose to go to the pizza parlor or to the deli.

A polarity, however, cannot be solved. It presents us not with a single challenge, but with two poles of a dilemma—neither of which will go away. Because the two sides of the issue are interdependent, we can't simply choose one as a solution while ignoring the other. The best we can do is manage a polarity by attempting to gain what is positive from each side while doing our best to minimize their limitations. Johnson also points out that each pole of the dilemma has its positive and negative characteristics, its up and down sides. Inevitably, the positive aspects of one pole will be the opposites of the other pole's negative traits.[2]

Let's take a known example. What to do about the welfare program is one of the great social problems facing our country. Yet the ongoing nature of the situation indicates that it is probably not a problem at all. Rather, it is a polarity. Personal responsibility forms one side of the equation while governmental support forms the other. The positive aspects of personal responsibility include individual initiative, resourcefulness, and a sense of obligation to provide for oneself and one's family. On the negative side it can foster communal callousness, inequality, selfishness, and isolation. The positive aspects of governmental support are communal responsibility, greater equality, sharing, and a sense of the common good. Its negatives include erosion of personal initiative, a sense of resignation, and a dependence on external means of support.

If we were to diagram these two poles we would get a figure like this:

	+	+
Individual Responsibility	Personal Initiative Resourcefulness Obligation to family and oneself	Communal responsibility Greater equality Sharing Common good	Governmental Support
	Communal callousness Inequality Selfishness Isolation –	Erosion of initiative Sense of resignation Dependence on aid from outside sources –	

An axiom of polarity management states that if you try to embrace solely the positives of one side you will inevitably also slip down into its negative characteristics. You will then need to move toward the positive elements of the other pole in an attempt to maximize the best characteristics of both sides. The history of welfare policy in this country reveals this dynamic to be true. Many Americans prospered under the ethic of "rugged individualism," but others, due to discrimination or lack of opportunity, were left behind. Programs like the Great Society of the Lyndon Johnson era helped bring additional Americans into the economic mainstream but engendered a cycle of dependence that has threatened to relegate parts of our nation into becoming a permanent underclass. The debate continues over how to restore individual responsibility with policies like workfare and time limits on welfare grants, while not cutting the safety net out from under those who truly cannot help themselves.

When applied to matters of the spirit, we can see that the dilemma of seeking or dwelling is not a problem, but a polarity (see opposite page). As expressed by the author's hope in Psalm 27, the most fulfilling type of religious expression is that which can embrace the positive aspects of both abiding in and visiting God's house at the same time.

Since our prior discussions have touched on both the pluses and minuses of dwelling and seeking, it might be helpful to summarize these in diagram form (see page 167).

Robert Wuthnow has suggested that there is a form of spirituality that might best manage the polarity of dwelling and seeking. He calls it the "spirituality of practice."[3] According to his definition, practice spirituality has the following characteristics:

- *Intentionality.* The spirituality of practice requires you to have a deep awareness of your own religious motives and objectives. Much

Dwelling		Seeking
+ Group identity Communal support Continuity and reliability Transmittability of values to next generation	+ Personal relationship with God Gaining wisdom from many traditions Respect for individual religious needs Entering into the mystery of God	
Organizational imperatives over individual needs Denominational exclusivity Enforced homogeneity Predictability of observance −	Rootlessness Isolation "Making it up as you go along" Idiosyncratic, nontransmittable nature of values and practice −	

of what regularly occurs at our religious institutions is done mechanically. Prayers are sung by rote; observances are performed by force of habit; rites are celebrated because others expect us to do so. These religious expressions do provide many with a sense of comfort and familiarity. However, the spirituality of practice requires more. It requires conscious choice. It does not stop at formalities that can represent a negative aspect of dwelling spirituality. It bids us to extract personal meaning from the scriptural tales we choose to read, to utter our prayers with the conviction of heartfelt petition, and to embrace contemplation as moments of encountering God or sensing our interconnectedness with all things. Practice spirituality would have us consciously open our eyes as we seek to discern the divine that underlies the circumstances and relationships of our lives.

- *Time and Deliberate Effort.* Just as serious athletes and chess masters need practice to become skillful in their chosen endeavors, so too is practice necessary to obtain the benefits of a spiritual life. Contrary to the reputation for browsing that is found in some forms of spiritual seeking, practice spirituality is not dabbling. You need to set aside regular time in your schedule for prayer, scriptural reading, meditation, or any other serious discipline. Rabbi Jonathan Omer-Mann, a leading Jewish spiritual teacher from Los Angeles, describes his own contemplative practice as "Noble Boredom."[4] While its goal is not to be tiresome, practice spirituality requires regular, sustained attention over time.

- *Communal Ties.* A sense of connection to others is a necessary complement to your personal search. Even those practicing solitary meditation don't act in a vacuum. A tradition was needed to transmit that practice. Books, teachers, and centers help to convey that practice today. Those who share in the quest and others whose lives will be touched in some way strengthen the seemingly solitary meditator. Spirituality is not an escape from family, community, and friends. Rather, it should lead to a more sanctified or mindful way of interacting with them.

- *Right Living.* More than feeling good, practice spirituality is about living a good life on a sustained basis. The Gospels indicate that "by their fruits you shall know them." Those who would invite God into their lives must reciprocate by allowing God to act through them by living ethically and performing loving acts.

At its best, interfaith spiritual direction can guide us toward a powerful expression of this spirituality of practice. It can help us embrace the religious poles of dwelling and seeking in a way that highlights the positive features while minimizing their drawbacks.

Interfaith spiritual direction is nothing if not intentional. The entire premise of spiritual direction is based on a conscious decision by the seeker to deepen his or her relationship with God or, in the case of Buddhists, to live more mindfully. Therefore, each relationship you have, each triumph and defeat you experience, each change of circumstance becomes an occasion to reflect on God's movement in your life or on how past experiences or fears of the future might be affecting your experience of the present.

As the seekers and guides we have met in these pages testify, our intentionality becomes magnified when we begin to see things from the perspective of another tradition. Suddenly we look at long-familiar texts, prayers, or customs from an entirely different point of view. Aspects of spiritual expression that might have been previously unknown to us or submerged within our own tradition can emerge with a freshness and vitality that can reorient our relationship to God and the world. Perfunctory religious observance and the mechanical performance of daily tasks are no longer options when we consciously walk with God.

Dedicated time and deliberate effort are also pre-requisites for spiritual guidance. While a guide might introduce a seeker to a variety of spiritual practices, these are not suggested randomly. Rather, they are selected deliberately to help seekers progressively grow and deepen their recognition of God's presence in their lives. Care is taken to prescribe scriptural passages or prayer exercises appropriate to the seeker's current need, be it for solace or to challenge pat assumptions. The seeker might then meditate on the same verse or perform a given practice for weeks or months at a time as its transformative effects slowly unfold.

A story from the Zen tradition perfectly illustrates this need for sustained practice that cannot be rushed.

> A novice asked his teacher how long it would take for him to become enlightened. "About ten years," replied the master.
> "And if I try really hard?" inquired the novice.
> "Then it will probably take you twenty," was the reply.[5]

Time and deliberation take on particular importance in interfaith direction. Patience and consideration are needed as new terminology, insights, and practices are introduced. If the religious traditions and boundaries of both the seeker and the guide are to be respected, care is needed as points of correspondence and difference are explored. Serious spiritual growth requires deliberate effort—not haphazard dabbling, trying on another faith's practice as if it were an exotic scarf to be modeled and then discarded.

I know from my own experiences that interfaith seekers can feel exuberant when faced with fresh religious discovery. The urge becomes strong to go faster, to move on to the next practice in hope of attaining even greater spiritual heights.

I was fortunate that my first director, Sister Elizabeth Hilman, was firm in checking those impulses and teaching me that in spiritual development, constancy and dedication over time are what count. When discussing my first attempts at meditation she would continually remind me, "Howard, you get credit simply by showing up and trying each day."

Although spiritual direction seems focused on the individual's quest for greater meaning, moral living and communal responsibility are its surest measures. How our perceptions of the world and interactions with others have changed give us more telling signs that we are being transformed than the depth of any contemplative state. As Claude d'Estrée reminds us, if you meditate for twenty-five years and still act like an S.O.B., something is seriously wrong. On the other hand, when you begin to see God's image reflected even in the faces of people you find annoying and consider duties that are troubling or burdensome to be spiritual tasks that open new avenues to growth, then the spirit is moving within you. Sharing in congregational worship and the obligation to help others all become part of the journey.

This broadening of ties to the community and to right living take on an added dimension through interfaith spiritual guidance. The ability to celebrate commonality and respect differences, to identify with our own traditions while feeling kinship and a responsibility to all creatures is a special blessing.

It can lead us to see life as a wheel with the sacred as the living hub and each of us as points along a common rim. As we move down our own spoke toward the core we begin to realize that as we come closer to the divine center we, of necessity, become closer to each other.

What is the promise of interfaith spiritual direction? That it can embrace the best aspects of the spirituality of seeking and the spirituality of dwelling; that by exposing us to another tradition's wisdom we can deepen our personal relationship with God, while maintaining, if not revitalizing, our ties to our own communities of faith.

What is the promise of interfaith spiritual direction? For Dale Rhodes it lies in, "Spiritual directors who are especially skilled in noticing the unique ways God manifests Godself. As we move into a religiously pluralistic society, spiritual directors have a special ability and calling to offer. Hopefully we can 'step up to the challenge' because we are already experienced in recognizing that the ultimate isn't perceived or felt the same by every individual."

What is the promise of interfaith spiritual direction? That by guiding us both to spiritually abide and to spiritually visit at the same time, it can guide each of us to form our own rooted yet searching spirituality of practice in the creative tension between the two poles.

In his study of polarity, Barry Johnson reminds us that even when you maximize the positive aspects of both poles the process is not complete. The movement between the two sides is constant. Since some slippage into the negative domain is inevitable, continuing care and adaptation is needed if the most positive possible results are to be obtained. The goal of polarity management is to limit movement between the negative aspects of the poles while maximizing the positive.

A diagram of this continuing process might look like this:

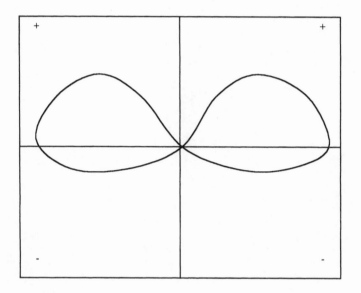

Interestingly enough, this figure looks like an infinity sign rising. Perhaps it symbolizes interfaith direction's greatest promise of all. By discovering with our guides how to hold both spiritual poles while dynamically moving between the two, our souls might continue to grow, rise even higher after their inevitable falls, and just maybe touch the infinite as well.

Epilogue

The Next Hundred Years: A Parable of Future Hope

Reb Aaron of Karlin bore the name of his grandfather, Reb Aaron the Great. And like his grandfather the second Reb Aaron served the Karliner Hasidism as their righteous leader, their *tzaddik*. Karlin held a special place within the galaxy of Hasidic courts, for it was the capital of ecstatic prayer.

With raised voices that rolled back clouds and pierced the skies, the Hasidim of Karlin joined their souls in fervent worship three times a day. One of their leaders, Reb Uri Strelisker, was even known as the Seraph, the fiery angel, due to the burning zeal of his prayer that threatened to consume his spirit at any moment.

One afternoon Reb Aaron felt troubled. He called together a few of his most trusted disciples to join him on a field trip. Their mission: to bolster their faith by offering a special rendition of *minchah,* the service of the dusk. Their destination—wherever the spirit might lead.

Piling into their carriage, Reb Aaron bid his driver to turn backwards, allowing the horses to run where they'd will. The journey went on and on until the hour of dusk was upon them.

"Rebbe," called the students, "the time for *minchah* has all but passed. Are we there yet?"

"Patience, my sons," replied the Rebbe, as the carriage and it horses flew down the road.

Hours and miles passed. The sky was pitch black and dusk was all but a distant memory. Again the students asked about their destination. Again the Rebbe told them to wait.

At one o'clock in the morning Reb Aaron, his disciples and the wagon pulled up in front of a small inn in the midst of an equally small backwater village.

"Ah, now we are here," sighed the Rebbe, "This is the place."

Alighting from his carriage the Rebbe knocked on the door. A wizened old man opened the portal; his eyes still clouded from sleep.

"May we come in?" asked Reb Aaron, "we would like to daven, to pray, the *minchah* service."

"Well, you're a little early for tomorrow afternoon, but come along."

Little did the innkeeper know what was about to happen, for he did not recognize that these guests of the night were Hasidim from Karlin. They gathered together and began worship with an introduction to Psalm 145:

HAPPY!!! ARE THEY!!! THAT DWELL IN YOUR HOUSE!!! THEY!!! WILL EVER PRAISE YOU!!! LORD!!!

The sound of their prayer was like crashing thunder. It woke all the good Christian villagers who lived in the surrounding streets. The villagers started with alarm, for the only time they heard such nocturnal screaming was when one of their structures caught fire, threatening both property and life. Grabbing their buckets they ran toward the source of the racket, the inn.

When they arrived they found the inn ablaze. But it burned with a different type of flame—the flame of intensely hot religious fervor. Not knowing what to do, the villagers put down their buckets and soon picked up the recitation of their own prayers. Jewish and Christian hymns echoed through the night urging each other higher and higher. Slowly the verses of praise began to soften until both groups concluded. The villagers shook hands with the Hasidim and went home to their beds.

As the disciples headed for the door, Reb Aaron turned back. A big, powerful man was Reb Aaron, and he lifted the innkeeper off the floor until the frail elder stood upon a table.

"Tell us what happened?" inquired the Rebbe.

"I don't know what you mean, Master," the innkeeper replied.

"Tell us what happened!" the Rebbe's voice cried out, this time with greater insistence.

Suddenly the innkeeper's eyes lightened, his lips raised in a wide smile, "Yes! Now I recall. You see—today is my one-hundred-and-eighth birthday. A century ago, I was but a little boy helping my father and grandfather care for the inn. On this night, at this hour, ten decades ago, an earlier sage knocked on our door. When we opened it we gaped with surprise, it was the holy Baal Shem Tov! Like you, he and his disciples gathered to offer the *minchah* prayers. Like my neighbors tonight, their forebears came rushing to the inn only to join their voices to those of the Baal Shem's Hasidim.

"Before he left, the Baal Shem Tov stood me upon this very table and asked me my age. When I told him it was my eighth birthday he looked deeply into my eyes.

'My precious son, know that exactly one hundred years from tonight a rebbe just like me will knock on your door. When my friend arrives, give him this message. Tell him that there was one who came here before him. And tell him that no matter what, when people of faith lift their voices together they can guide each other, their prayers can join to heal the fissures in heaven itself!'"

Slowly Reb Aaron returned to his carriage. Reassured with hope for the future, he wondered: Who might come to join their prayerful voices together during the next hundred years and beyond?[1]

Resources for Spiritual direction

As mentioned in Chapter 6, the first place you should check in your quest for spiritual guidance is your local church, mosque, synagogue, temple, or ashram. If spiritual direction is not offered there, someone might be able to help you with a suitable reference. Other avenues to explore include local hospital chaplaincies, campus religious foundations, retreat centers, and renewal movements. Many of these can be found in the phone book.

The following list contains sources to explore among the individual faith traditions as well as descriptions of some ecumenical and interfaith centers. Because no complete list of interfaith centers has been compiled, I welcome information about other such institutions that might be included in future editions.

Remember, your search for the right spiritual director might not be easy. In addition to the issue of finding an appropriate match, some directors and denominations feel comfortable offering guidance only to members of their own faith or to those who express serious interest in conversion. Don't despair. Maintaining faith and optimism during your search is also an avenue for spiritual growth.

Interfaith/Ecumenical

The Shalem Institute for Spiritual Formation
5430 Grosvenor Lane
Bethesda, MD 20814
(301) 897-7334
www.shalem.org

Dedicated to Christian contemplative spirituality, Shalem draws upon the wisdom of other traditions and welcomes people of all backgrounds. Offering a variety of spiritual deepening programs and spiritual direction groups in the Baltimore/Washington area, Shalem also offers extension programs in spiritual direction, contemplative group leadership, personal spiritual deepening, and spirituality for executives. The Shalem Fellowship counts among its members spiritual directors throughout North America who have trained with Shalem under the direction of its Program Director, Sister Rose Mary Dougherty.

Spiritual Directors International (SDI)
1329 Seventh Avenue
San Francisco, CA 94122
(415) 566-1560
www.sdiworld.org

SDI has a membership roster of over 3,300 spiritual directors. While the vast majority of them are Christian, guides from other traditions and interfaith guides represent a newly growing segment of the SDI membership. Because SDI is organized in regions representing 110 different geographic areas of the world, its office can offer referrals to directors around the globe.

Regional

Center for Spiritual Practice and Counseling
631 Clay Street
Ashland, OR 97520
(541) 512-9071
spiritcenter@juno.com

Dr. Mary Ann Woodman maintains a full-time interfaith spiritual guidance practice with offices in Oregon and California. A Roman Catholic, she has learned and draws upon the spiritual tools of other traditions stemming from her involvement in interfaith spirituality dating back to the 1960s. Entering into discernment with seekers on their spiritual terms, her practice includes seekers of Christian, Jewish, Sufi, Buddhist, and Hindu traditions.

Interfaith Spiritual Center
3910 S.E. 11th Avenue
Portland, OR 97202
(503) 233-2026

Founded by Cecilia Ranger, SNJM, Ph.D., in 1998, the I.S.C. staff includes members from Jewish, Catholic, Taoist, and Unitarian Universalist traditions. Individual, family, and group spiritual direction are offered, as are retreats and workshops on the spiritual life and practice of the major world religions. Introductory public classes on Eastern and Western spirituality are presented on the first Wednesday of each month.

Interweave
P. O. Box 1516
Summit, NJ 07901
(973) 763-8312

Founded in 1974, Interweave is dedicated to helping people of all backgrounds find spirituality, wellness, and the common good. Its public offerings include programs and workshops in aspects of Christian, Jewish, and interfaith spirituality. Interweave's founder, Reverend Bob Morris, an Episcopal priest, has offered guidance to

Jewish, Muslim, and Christian seekers, and can offer interfaith referrals to guides in the New York, New Jersey, and Philadelphia areas.

Resources for Ecumenical Spirituality
Forest House
3704 Highway 13
Dunnegan, MO 65640
(417) 754-2562
resecum@hotmail.com

RES seeks to foster mutual understanding among religious faiths through shared spiritual practice and dialogue. RES retreats, colloquia, and workshops are offered in the Missouri/Minnesota/Illinois area as well as in other parts of North America. Spiritual guidance is offered by visit, mail, or phone. Among those offering interfaith spiritual direction is Mary Jo Meadow, OCDS, a Catholic sister who has also taken the precepts of a Theravada Buddhist nun, and who has over forty years of meditation experience in three different traditions.

Shem Center for Interfaith Spirituality
316 Lake Street
Oak Park, IL 60302
(708) 848-1095
http://members.aol.com/SHEMcenter

Founded during the 1993 Parliament of World Religions, the Shem Center welcomes sojourners from all spiritual paths interested in experiencing and celebrating the spiritual expressions of all world religions. In addition to lectures and classes, the center sponsors experiential day programs and retreats. Its director, Brother Joseph Kilikevice, offers spiritual companioning to people from various backgrounds open to gleaning insights from other traditions and can offer referrals within the Chicago/Midwest area.

Tacheria: A Multifaith Centre for Spirituality
Reconciliation and the Sacred Arts
4440 North Campbell Avenue
Tuscon, AZ 85718
(502) 299-0498

Tacheria serves the entire southwestern United States
offering lectures, seminars, retreats, and spiritual guidance for people of all backgrounds. Founded by Dr.
Jeanette Renouf and Claude d'Estrée, Tacheria sponsors
the New School for Spiritual Directors, a unique two-year
multifaith training program in the art of spiritual direction.

The Tonglen Foundation
Claude d'Estrée
10816 Colton Street
Fairfax, VA 22032
(703) 591-3056
destree@worldnet.att.net

For an in-depth description of Claude's approach to interfaith spiritual direction, please see Chapter 8.

BUDDHISM

Those seeking Buddhist spiritual guidance would do well
to consult the book *The Complete Guide to Buddhist
America,* edited by Don Morreale (Boston: Shambhala
Publications, 1997), It contains an extensive list of the various movements and guides available.

CHRISTIANITY

Since spiritual direction among Christian denominations
is far and away the most prevalent in North America,
the organizations listed above under Ecumenical and
Interfaith should be able to refer you to Christian spiritual
directors representing a wide range of backgrounds and
orientations.

HINDUISM

The Vedanta Society of New York
34 West 71st Street
New York, NY 10023
(212) 877-9197
www.westved.org

The Vedanta Society's guidance reflects the more universalist approach to Hinduism taught by Sri Ramakrishna. Vedanta centers can also be found in several major cities throughout North America and Europe.

The Self-Realization Fellowship
3880 San Rafael Avenue
Los Angeles, CA 90065
(323) 225-2471
www.yogananda-srf.org

Based on the teachings of Paramahansa Yogananda, the Fellowship has branches in several North American cities.

ISLAM

The Haqqani Center
P. O. Box 1065
Fenton, Michigan, 48430
(810) 714-2296

Associated with the Naqshbandi order of Sufism, this center maintains ties with other Sufi orders throughout the world.

JUDAISM

Those seeking basic instruction in Judaism might contact local synagogues, Jewish community centers, or Jewish federations. Because spiritual direction in Orthodox Judaism is usually limited to those already Jewish and observant, and is just in its early stages in the more liberal denominations, you can contact me at *rabbia@juno.com* if you seek a referral.

NOTES

Chapter 1: Brewing Spirits

1. Adapted from Martin Buber, *Tales of the Hasidim: The Later Masters* (New York: Schocken Books, 1948), p. 250.

Chapter 2: Seekers

1. The Self-Realization Fellowship was founded in 1920. For more information see Paramahansa Yogananda, *Autobiography of a Yogi* (Los Angeles: Self-Realization Fellowship, 1993).
2. Lisa Miller, "The Age of Divine Disunity," *The Wall Street Journal.*
3. Richard Cimino and Don Lattin, "Religion," *American Demographics,* April 1999, p. 64–65.
4. Ibid., p. 63.
5. Cited in Robert Wuthnow, *After Heaven: Spirituality in America Since the 1950s* (Berkeley, Calif.: University of California Press, 1998), p. 74–75.
6. Lisa Miller, op. cit.
7. Umberto Cassuto, *The Goddess Anath* (Jerusalem: Magnes Press, 1971).
8. A. L. Basham, R. N. Dandekar, Peter Hardy, V. Raghauan and R. Weiler, *Sources of Indian Tradition,* Vol. I (New York: Columbia University Press, 1958), p. 53.
9. Ibid., p. 93, 107, 91.
10. Michael Barnes, "Masters and Mastery of Zen," in Lavinia Byrne, *Traditions of Spiritual Guidance* (Collegeville, Minn.: Liturgical Press, 1998), p. 181.
11. James B. Pritchard, ed., *The Ancient Near East* (Princeton, N.J.: Princeton University Press, 1958), p. 62.

12. See Moshe Idel, *Kabbalah: New Perspectives* (New Haven: Yale University Press, 1988), p. 9, 13, 15; and G. G. Scholem, *Kabbalah* (New York: New York Times Books, 1974), p. 25, 27, 35, 49.
13. A. J. Heschel, *The Prophets, Volume II* (New York: Harper and Row, 1962), chapter one.
14. John 1:29.
15. For a key confrontation between Elijah and the Prophet of Baal over this issue see 1 Kings 18.
16. Wuthnow, op. cit., p. 58.
17. Ibid., p. 36.
18. Lisa Miller, op. cit.
19. Wuthnow, op. cit., p. 7–10.

Chapter 3: What Is Spiritual Direction?

1. Carol Ochs and Kerry Olitzky, *Jewish Spiritual Guidance* (San Francisco: Jossey-Bass, 1997), p. 11.
2. Proverbs 19:21
3. John Renard, "Spiritual Guidance in Islam, II," in Lavinia Byrne, op. cit., p. 202.
4. Exodus 17:2.
5. Exodus 32:1.
6. Tilden Edwards, *Spiritual Friend* (Mahwah, N.J.: Paulist Press, 1980), p. 44.
7. Ibid., p. 45–46.
8. Genesis 4:17.
9. Exodus 16:3 and Leviticus 18:3.
10. Deuteronomy 8:2–3.
11. Jeremiah 2:2.
12. Benedicta Ward, "Spiritual Direction in the Desert Fathers," in Byrne, op. cit., p. 6.
13. Ibid., p. 8.
14. Ibid., p. 5.
15. Tilden Edwards, op. cit., p. 56–57.
16. Ibid., p. 60.
17. Mary Beth McCauley, "Guides Who Help Find God in Daily Life," *The Philadelphia Inquirer,* October 11, 1998, p. H7.
18. Charles T. Tart, Ph.D., in Helen Palmer, *The Enneagram* (San Francisco: HarperSanFrancisco, 1988), p. x.
19. Thomas Merton quoted in *Spiritual Friend*, op. cit., p. 129.
20. Cathy Lynn Grossman, "The Unique Journey of Spiritual Companioning," *USA Today*, August 11, 1998, Final Edition, p. 8D.

21. McCauley, op. cit.
22. McCauley, op. cit.
23. Rose Mary Dougherty, *Group Spiritual Direction* (Mahwah, N.J.: Paulist Press, 1995), p. 20.
24. Ochs and Olitzky, op. cit., p. 74–76.
25. Ibid., p. 77–79.
26. Dougherty, op. cit., p. 44–45.

Chapter 4: Looking Beyond Your Own Faith

1. For a study of this congregation and its neighborhood see Louis Rosen, *The Southside* (Chicago: Ivan R. Dee, 1998).
2. Genesis 17:1.
3. My own search for a spiritual director came fully three years before the appearance of Kerry Olitzky's and Carol Ochs' fine book *Jewish Spiritual Guidance,* op. cit.
4. The Enneagram is a star-like figure that maps nine basis personality types and the dynamic interaction among these different personality styles. For further information see my book, *The Enneagram and Kabbalah: Reading Your Soul* (Woodstock, Vt.: Jewish Lights, 1998).
5. *Sources of Indian Tradition,* op. cit., p. 103–105.
6. 2 Kings 5:9–19.
7. Matthew 15:21–28.
8. Urban T. Holmes, *A History of Christian Spirituality* (Louisville, Ky.: Westminster Press, 1984).
9. Corrine Ware, *Discover Your Spiritual Type* (Bethesda, Md.: Alban Institute, 1995).
10. Lawrence Kushner, *God Was In This Place and I, I Did Not Know* (Woodstock, Vt.: Jewish Lights, 1991), p. 28.
11. Rodger Kamenetz, *The Jew in the Lotus* (San Francisco: HarperSanFrancisco, 1994)
12. *After Heaven,* op. cit., p. 91.
13. *Spiritual Friend,* op. cit., p. 117.
14. Zalman Schachter-Shalomi, *Spiritual Intimacy* (Northvale, N.J.: Jason Aronson Inc., 1996), p. 136. A full discussion of this form of spiritual guidance can be found in section 5 of this text, "Techniques and Resources of the Yachidut."
15. Louis Ginsberg, "Rabbi Israel Salanter" in Judah Goldin, ed., *The Jewish Expression* (New York: Bantam Books, 1970), p. 415–447.

16. Paul Jackson, "Spiritual Guidance in Islam, I," in *Traditions of Spiritual Guidance,* op. cit., p. 188–189.

17. Ibid., p. 196.

18. John Renard, "Spiritual Guidance in Islam, II," in *Traditions of Spiritual Guidance,* op. cit., p. 209.

19. Ibid., p. 207.

20. Bawa Muhaiyaddeen, *Sheikh and Disciple* (Philadelphia: Bawa Muhaiyaddeen Fellowship, 1983), p. 17, 48, 78.

21. *Sources of Indian Tradition,* op. cit., p. 99.

22. Michael Barnes, "Masters and Mastery in Zen," in *Traditions of Spiritual Guidance,* op. cit. p. 177.

23. Ibid., p. 186.

Chapter 5: Blessings and Drawbacks

1. Psalms 118:17—The usual reading is "I shall not die but live to recount the works of the Lord."

2. On the benefits of having a spiritual director who is not of your denomination's hierarchy see *Spiritual Friend,* op. cit., p. 118.

3. Beatrice Bruteau, "Insight and Manifestation: A Way of Prayer in a Christian Context," in *Contemplative Review,* Fall 1983, p. 20.

4. Psalm 19:34.

5. Aryeh Kaplan, *Jewish Meditation* (New York: Schocken, 1985), p. 56; and Yitzhak Buxbaum, *Jewish Spiritual Practices* (Northvale, N.J.: Jason Aronson, 1990), p. 443.

6. Louis Jacobs, *Jewish Mystical Testimonies* (New York: Schocken, 1977), p. 73–74.

7. Babylonian Talmud, Tractate Chagigah 140.

8. Lisa Miller, "The Age of Divine Disunity," *The Wall Street Journal.*

9. Rose Mary Dougherty, *Group Spiritual Direction,* op. cit., p. 22–23.

10. See Tony Schwartz, *What Really Matters* (New York: Bantam Books, 1996), p. 89–90.

11. Ibid., p. 307.

12. Ibid., p. 333.

13. *Spiritual Friend,* op. cit., p. 108–111.

14. Christian Cabala represents the attempt by certain non-normative Christian spiritualists to correlate aspects of Christianity to the symbols of Jewish mysticism (this is usually differentiated by the spelling *kabbalah*). Among the more notable early figures in this movement was the seventeenth-century Jesuit Athanasius Kircher.

Chapter 6: Where Shall the Seeker Search?

1. "Spiritual Guidance in Islam, I," op. cit., p. 197.
2. "Spiritual Guidance in Islam, II," op. cit., p. 208–209.
3. *Pirke Avot* (Ethics of the Fathers).
4. *Group Spiritual Direction,* op. cit., p. 9–11.
5. Ibid., p. 38–48.
6. Ibid., p. 35–36.
7. *Spiritual Friend,* op. cit., p. 174–176.
8. "Spiritual Guidance in Islam, I," op. cit., p. 198. For a full discussion of the factors to consider when searching for a guide see *Spiritual Friend,* ibid., chapter 5 "Seeking a spiritual friend."
9. Ochs and Olitzky, *Jewish Spiritual Guidance,* op. cit., p. 3.
10. "Guides who help . . ." *Philadelphia Inquirer,* op. cit.
11. For further information see David L. Fleming, *Modern Spiritual Exercises* (Garden City, N.Y.: Image Books, 1978), which provides a contemporary approach to the seminal work on discernment, and *The Spiritual Exercises* by the sixteenth-century founder of the Jesuit Order, Saint Ignatius of Loyola.

Chapter 7: Contemporary Spiritual Trends

1. Babylonian Talmud, Yoma 9b.
2. Tony Schwartz, *What Really Matters: Searching for Wisdom in America* (New York: Bantam Books, 1995).
3. Ibid., p. 431–432.
4. Isaac Husik, *A History of Medieval Jewish Philosophy* (New York: Meridan Books, 1958), p. 312.
5. William T. DeBary, Wing-Tsit Chan and Burton Watson, eds., *Sources of Chinese Tradition,* volume I (New York: Columbia University, 1964), p. 277–278. While the name Confucius (b. 551 BCE) is known beyond students of China, the other figures mentioned in this extract are probably not. Mencius, or Meng Tzu (b. 372), studied with a disciple of Confucius' grandson and is known in China as the Second Sage. Yao and Shun were sage-kings who reigned around the twenty-second century BCE and whose sayings figure prominently in later Confucian writings. The Duke of Chou, who lived in the eleventh-century BCE, served as regent to the third king of the Chou dynasty and was portrayed as a paragon of virtue by Confucius. Scholarly debate still exists over the identity of the Buddhist protagonist Mou Tzu.

6. See John Herman Randall, *Hellenistic Ways of Deliverance and the Making of the Christian Synthesis* (New York: Columbia University Press, 1970).
7. Benjamin Barber, *Jihad vs. McWorld* (New York: Ballantine Books, 1995), p. 212–213.

Chapter 9: The Modern Spiritual Paradox

1. Barry Johnson, *Polarity Management* (Amherst, Mass.: HRD Press, 1992).
2. Ibid., p. xii.
3. Robert Wuthnow, *After Heaven,* op. cit., chapter 7.
4. Avram Davis, ed., *Meditation from the Heart of Judaism: Today's Teachers Share Their Practices, Techniques, and Faith* (Woodstock, Vt.: Jewish Lights, 1997), p. 75.
5. Michael Barnes, "Masters and Mastery of Zen," op. cit., p. 180.

Epilogue: The Next Hundred Years

1. I first heard a version of this tale from Neshama Carlebach, daughter of the late musician and teacher, Rabbi Shlomo Carlebach, at a Sabbath retreat in the Colorado Rockies during the summer of 1998.

I was privileged to repeat it some months later on Yom Kippur afternoon. The Archbishop of Philadelphia, His Eminence Anthony Cardinal Bevilaqua, had come to our synagogue on our holiest day to offer words of reconciliation based on the recent papal letter, "Shoah, We Remember the Holocaust." It was with this story that I introduced the Cardinal to the 1,500 worshippers who came to hear his words and join their voices in memory and prayer with his.

GLOSSARY

BUDDHIST TERMS

dharma—Cosmic law of righteousness as well as the qualities and characteristics manifest in all phenomena. Identified with the teachings of the Buddha.

kalyanamitra—Literally "friend of the heart." A spiritual companion or friend.

koan—A paradoxical, puzzling, or nonsensical statement used to push the mind beyond the limits of cognitive reason.

löpon—Master teacher.

mantra—Meditation practice involving the repetition of mystical syllables or phrases.

mudra—Ritual gesture of the hands in Buddhist meditation practice—as seen in much Buddhist statuary.

nirvana—"Cessation" of entanglement or attachement. The state of supreme bliss in which individual ego ceases to exist.

roshi—Elder or master in Zen.

samadhi—Meditative absorption achieved through *samatha* practice. Distinction between the subject and object disappears.

samatha—Meditation that focuses concentration on a single point.

satori—Experience or state of enlightenment.

sutra—A Buddhist scripture.

vipassana—Insight meditation.

zazen—The sitting meditation practice of Zen.

BUDDHIST NAMES

Dalai Lama—Spiritual and temporal head of Tibetan Buddhism. His Holiness, Tenzin Gyatso is the fourteenth Dalai Lama, currently living in exile in Northern India.

Hakuin (1685–1768)—Japanese Zen master who taught the reaching of enlightenment through meditation on *koans*.

Menander—Greek king who ruled in northwestern India during the middle of the second century BCE. Alleged to have converted to Buddhism, he minted the Buddhist symbol of the wheel on his coins.

Nagasena—Buddhist monk whose spiritual direction and public debates influenced Menander.

CHRISTIAN TERMS

Abba—Aramaic for *father*. Title of male spiritual leaders of the Desert Fathers. Female equivalent is *Amma*.

Cursillo Movement—Begun in Spain in 1949, this movement sponsors three-day retreats with the goal of leading retreat participants to an encounter with Christ.

Desert Fathers—Name applied to teachers and saints of the early Christian monastic movement that existed from the end of the third through the beginning of the fifth centuries CE. These monks lived alone or in ascetic groups in the deserts of Egypt, Syria, and Judea.

Jesus Prayer—The practice of continuous repetetive prayer originating between the fifth and eighth centuries CE, and commonly found throughout the Eastern Orthodox Church. Based on Saint Paul's injunction, "Pray without ceasing" (I Thessalonians 5:17). The most common form is "Lord Jesus Christ, Son of God, have mercy on me, a sinner."

poustinikki—Hermits of the Russian Orthodox tradition who offered counsel and intercessory prayer.

staretz—Literally "elder." A spiritual father in the Eastern Orthodox tradition.

Christian Names

Abba Antony (250–353 CE)—Egyptian Desert Father, considered the father of the hermits.

Abba Arsenius—Fourth-century CE Desert Father of Scetis in Egypt.

Eddy, Mary Baker—Nineteenth-century founder of the Christian Science Movement.

Ignatius Loyola (1491–1556)—Founder of the Society of Jesus (Jesuits) and author of *The Spiritual Exercises*.

John of the Cross (1542–1591)—Spanish Carmelite mystic and reformer. Author of *The Dark Night of the Soul*.

Merton, Thomas (1915–1968)—Trappist monk who explored the relationship between Christianity and Buddhism.

Pennington, M. Basil—Twentieth-century Trappist monk who was one of the originators of centering prayer, a modern contemplative practice in Christianity.

Teresa of Ávila (1515–1582)—Spanish Carmelite nun who was both a great mystic and reformer. Author of *The Interior Castle* and many other works.

Thomas Aquinas (1225–1274)—Dominican priest who is considered the most influential of Catholic philosophers. Incorporated Aristotelian perspectives into traditional Christian theology.

Saint Seraphim of Sarov (1759–1833)—Most famous Russian saint of the nineteenth century, he was a staretz and a monk.

Stein, Edith—Twentieth-century German philosopher of Jewish descent who became a Carmelite nun. During the Second World War she was imprisoned in Auschwitz where she died.

Hindu Terms

atman—The real or true self that underlies and is present in human experience.

avatar—An incarnation of the Divine.

Bhagavad-Gita—Literally "The Song of the Lord," a fourth-century BCE Sanskrit text considered a quintessential expression of some aspects of Hindu philosophy. It is part of the long epic poem *Mahabharata*.

Brahman—The impersonal Absolute, beyond attributes, that is the origin and support of the visible universe.

Brahmin—The Hindu priestly caste, the highest social order.

darshan—Homage given to a guru. Can also apply to the homage or respect shown to a holy image or place.

dharma—The moral law that sustains the world, human society, and the individual.

guru—Spiritual teacher or preceptor.

karma—The law of consequence with regard to action that is the driving force behind the cycle of reincarnation or rebirth.

Mogul—The Muslim empire established by conquest in India beginning in the sixteenth century CE.

moksha—Release from the cycle of transmigration of the soul.

puja—Worship, including the wide range of rituals that express it, such as placing an offering of flowers, lights, or food before a holy image.

sadhu—A wandering renunciant.

samsara—The cycle of transmigration of the soul: its birth, death, and rebirth.

swami—Member of a monastic order.

Vedanta Society—Spiritual movement started by Swami Vivekananda based on the teachings of Ramakrishna.

Vedas—The four collections of writings that are the foundation of all Hindu scripture.

Vishnu—The preserver god who, along with Brahma the creator and Shiva the destroyer, make up the "trinity." Embodiment of goodness and mercy, and the supreme god for Hindu Vaishnavites, Vishnu is thought to have had numerous incarnations, including Krishna.

yoga—Literally "yoke." A system for controlling mind and body through physical, ethical, devotional, or contemplative disciplines.

Hindu Names

Paramahansa Yogananda (1893–1952)—Indian teacher who taught widely in the West, first coming to America in 1920.

Ramakrishna (1836–1886)—Indian sage who taught the universal validity of all religions. Considered by his devotees to be an *avatar* (incarnation) of the Divine.

Sai Baba (b. 1926)—Believed by his followers to be an *avatar,* a divine incarnation on a par with spiritual leaders such as Krishna, Buddha, or Jesus. His name means "Divine Mother and Father."

Sri Aurobindo (1872–1950)—A twentieth-century Vedantic yogin and philosopher whose writings are still widely read among Hindus and others, and whose ashram remains active in Pondicherry, south India.

Swami Vivekananda (1863–1902)—Disciple of Ramakrishna who brought the Vedanta movement to Europe and America.

Maharishi Mahesh Yogi—Indian teacher who originated the practice of Transcendental Meditation.

ISLAMIC TERMS

chilla—A forty-day supervised retreat.

dhikr—Literally "the remembrance of God." The chanting of the divine names and attributes, often done in a group.

futuwah—"Spiritual chivalry," the second level of spiritual development in Sufism.

irfan—The highest stage of Sufi spiritual growth, only achieved under the spiritual direction of a sheikh. Mystical knowledge of God, gnosis.

husn al-adab—"Proper demeanor." Behavioral criteria used by a sheikh to determine growth of a disciple.

husn az-zann—"Thinking well" of God. Attitudinal criteria reflecting gratitude and transcending of egocentrism as a measure of a disciple's spiritual growth.

jihad—Struggle against moral evil. When translated as "holy war" it refers to the outer "lesser struggle." When referring to the inner moral development it is known as the "greater struggle."

jinn—Good and bad psychic spirits or angels.

Koran—The holy scriptures of Islam, considered to be the literal word of God that was revealed over a period of twenty-three years to the prophet Muhammad and formally canonized in 651 BCE.

muruwah—Initial stage of religious moral development open to all believers.

shariah—Islamic law stemming from the Koran detailing every aspect of a Muslim's life.

sheikh—Sufi spiritual guide.

shirk—Idolatry or polytheism.

Sufism—Mystical movement in Islam that traces its origin back to the Prophet Muhammad and his companions. Its name is derived from the woolen garment worn by its adherents. The Naqshbandi order was formalized as a distinct branch of Sufism during the twelfth century in central Asia.

ISLAMIC NAMES

Al-farabi (d. 950)—Islamic philosopher of the Baghdad school who used Aristotelian arguments to prove the existence of God.

Averroes (1126–1198)—Born in Cordoba and known for his philosophical commentaries on the works of Aristotle.

Avicenna (980–1037)—Philosopher born in Persia whose originality of thought was influenced by Aristotelianism and Neoplatonism.

Bawa Muhaiyaddeen (?–1986)—Twentieth-century Sufi sheikh from Sri Lanka who came to the United States in 1971 and remained there to teach. His later years were spent in Philadelphia.

Ibn'Abbad (1330–1390)—Sufi sheikh and guide born in Spain who spent most of his life in Morocco.

Sharafuddin Maneri (1290–1381)—Indian-born Sufi sheikh and spiritual guide.

JUDAIC TERMS

Ayn Sof—Literally "Without End." Used in kabbalah to describe the boundless, unknowable God.

bar/bat mitzvah—The age at which a Jewish boy or girl reaches the age of religious responsibility; and by extension, the ceremony celebrating the achievement of this status. For a boy, this occurs at age thirteen and for a girl, between the age of twelve and thirteen.

bentchen zich—Yiddish term for giving a blessing. Used to describe a private meeting between a hasid and a rebbe.

challah—Special Sabbath and holiday loaves of bread, usually braided for year-round use and circular for High Holy Day use.

chevruta—Dyads of students in a yeshiva setting who come together primarily for study but also for spiritual companioning.

daven—Yiddish word meaning "to pray."

Din—God's attribute of judgment.

Essenes—Jews of the second century BCE through the first century CE who conformed their lives to the ascetic world-view of the Qumran community without living permanently within the community.

etzah—"Advice," used to describe the insight and direction that the rebbe will convey to the Hasid toward the end of their meeting.

Etz Chayim—The "Tree of Life," which refers to a kabbalistic configuration of the ten manifestations of God's personality *(sefirot)*.

gerushin—Literally "to divorce or send away." Applied to a form of mantra-like meditation that banishes all distractions.

Hasidim—Popular mystical and pietist movement founded in Eastern Europe by Rabbi Israel Baal Shem Tov (d. 1759).

hitlahavut—Burning religious enthusiasm or zeal.

kabbalah—Jewish mystical tradition. When spelled *cabala* it is mostly used to describe a form of antinomian Christian or occult spiritualism based on Jewish mystical teachings.

kvittel—"A note" upon which one writes a request to give to the rebbe. Also applied to petitionary notes placed in the Western Wall in Jerusalem.

machshavah zarah—An "alienating thought" that distracts our concentration during study, prayer, or meditation. Sometimes has the connotation of a sexual fantasy.

malach—Hebrew term for an angel, literally translates as "messenger."

Malachi—Last of the Hebrew prophets, he lived during the fifth century BCE.

mashgiach—Literally a "supervisor." While most commonly applied to one who monitors the preparation of kosher food, also applies to the spiritual director at a yeshiva.

mashpia—A spiritual prompter in a Hasidic community who assists the community's leader, the rebbe, in the work of instruction and spiritual guidance.

menorah—Originally the seven-branched candelabrum used in Solomon's Temple. Popularly used to describe the nine-branched candelabrum of Hanukkah.

mincha—The afternoon service usually recited at dusk.

mitzvot—Ethical and ritual obligations incumbent upon Jews. Singular is *mitzvah,* commandment.

Musar—Ethicist movement in Judaism founded in Lithuania and Germany by Rabbi Israel Salanter in the mid-nineteenth century.

niggun—A wordless melody or chant.

pegisha—"Encounter," used to describe the rebbe/Hasid meeting.

penimiyut—Hebrew term for inwardness or the interior essence of things. Contrasted in kabbalistic and Hasidic writings with *chitzoniyut,* outer appearances.

Qumran—Area near the Dead Sea where the ascetic community credited with producing the Dead Sea Scrolls lived during the last century BCE until the destruction of the Second Temple in 70 CE.

rebbe—Title used for leader of Hasidic community. Has the connotation of one who attains leadership through the gift of divine charism, as opposed to the *rav* or rabbi whose authority is based on Talmudic acumen.

Rimmon—Ancient Syrian deity.

ruchaniyut—Hebrew term for spirituality found primarily in Hasidic writings. Usually contrasted with *gashmiyut,* physical reality and desire.

Samaria—Capital of the Northern Kingdom of Israel composed of the ten tribes that seceded from the Davidic dynasty following Solomon's death. Now sometimes applied to the entire northern Israelite kingdom.

sefirot—The ten manifestations of God's personality. Singular is *sefirah*.

Shechinah—God's nearness and immanence, identified in kabbalah as a feminine aspect of God and the tenth of the *sefirot*.

shmoozim—Talks delivered, often before holidays, by a yeshiva *mashgiach* (spiritual supervisor) on aspects of Judaism, observance, and the inner life.

Talmud—Main compilation of Jewish law and lore whose earliest section, the Mishna, was formalized in 200 CE in the land of Israel and whose later section, the Gemara, was redacted past the seventh century in the Persian Empire.

Torah—Scroll containing the Five Books of Moses.

tzaddik—Literally "the righteous one." Title given to the leaders of the various Hasidic communities.

yarmulke—A scullcap worn as a sign of respect to God. Also referred to in Hebrew as a *kippah*.

yechidut—"Coming together as one." Applied to one-on-one meeting of Rebbe and Hasid.

yeshiva—Talmudic academy, arguably the central institution of Orthodox Judaism. Plural is *yeshivot*.

JUDAIC NAMES

Aaron of Karlin—Nineteenth-century Hasidic master and leader of the Karlin dynasty. Bore same name as his grandfather who founded the dynasty in the late eighteenth century.

Joseph Gikatilla—Thirteenth-century Spanish kabbalist whose works include *The Gates of Light*.

Abraham Joshua Heschel (1907–1972)—European-born philosopher, author, and social activist who was rescued from Nazism and came to America during the 1940s. He bore the same name as his forbear, the nineteenth-century Hasidic leader Abraham Joshua Heschel of Apt.

Baal Shem Tov (1700–1760)—Literally "Master of the Good name," Rabbi Israel ben Eliezer, founding teacher of European Hasidism.

Moses Maimonides (1135–1204)—Leading medieval Jewish philosopher, legalist, and physician. Born in Spain, he later migrated to Egypt.

Uri Strelisker (d. 1826)—Hasidic master identified with the Karlin school of ecstatic prayer. He was known as the Seraph, fiery angel, due to the burning zeal of his worship.

ADDITIONAL TERMS

Aikido—A Japanese martial art.

Confucianism—Chinese doctrine advocating the embrace of humanity, benevolence, and virtue over profit and utilitarian gain. Founded by Confucius (K'ung Fu-tzu, b. 551 BCE), this teaching was first intended for those aspiring to political leadership but later extended throughout Chinese society.

Enneagram—A star-like figure that maps nine basic personality types and their dynamic interaction. This symbol was first introduced to the West by the Armenian-born philosopher George I. Gurdjieff (1847–1949).

Jainism—An Indian tradition that considers all elements, plants, and creatures to possess souls. Highly nonviolent and strictly vegetarian, its founding teacher was Mahavira (d. 468 BCE).

Taoism—A Chinese philosophy based upon the existence of an underlying principle, Tao, the Way, which is the source and governor of all beings and the core unity in which all contradictions and distinctions are resolved. Its first teachers were the possibly legendary Lao Tzu, to whom is attributed the text, *Tao-te Ching,* and the philosopher/recluse Chung Tzu (369–286 BCE).

ADDITIONAL NAMES

Cicero (106–43 BCE)—Roman statesman and orator who stressed the ideal of fellowship and that moral concepts proceed from our nature.

Duke of Chou—Regent to the King Ch'eng, virtuous founder of the Chou dynasty in the late twelfth century BCE.

Mencius (372–289 BCE)—The revitalizer of Confucianism and considered to be China's second sage.

Mou-Tzu (470–391 BCE)—Chinese philosopher who advocated practice of universal love by satisfying the material needs of others. Mouism for a time rivaled Confucian thought in China.

Pythagoras—Greek philosopher of sixth century BCE whose teachings described reality in terms of arithmetical relationships.

Seneca (d. 65 CE)—Roman philosopher, political leader, and author.

Shun—Semi-divine culture hero considered first to have taught the Chinese the arts of civilization.

Yao—Legendary Chinese figure of exceptional wisdom and virtue. Together with Shun and the Duke of Chou, is held up by Confucianism as model of a virtuous ruler.

Recommended Reading

American Spiritual Trends

Roof, Wade Clark, et al. *A Generation of Seekers*. San Francisco: HarperSanFrancisco, 1995.

Schwartz, Tony. *What Really Matters: Searching for Wisdom in America*. New York: Bantam Books, 1995.

Wuthnow, Robert. *After Heaven: Spirituality in America Since 1950*. Berkeley: University of California Press, 1998.

Religious Traditions— Introductory Texts

Buddhism

Kornfeld, Jack. *A Path with Heart*. New York: Bantam, 1993.

Rahula, Walpola. *What Buddha Taught*. New York: Grove Press, 1959.

Wilson-Ross, Nancy. *Buddhism: A Way of Life and Thought*. New York: Vintage, 1981.

Christianity

Alexander, Donald, ed. *Christian Spirituality: Five Views of Sanctification*. Downers Grove, Ill.: Intervarsity Press, 1988.

Cox, Michael. *Handbook of Christian Spirituality*. San Francisco: Harper and Row, 1985.

Holt, Bradley P. *Thirsty for God*. Minneapolis: Augsburg Books, 1993.

Hinduism

Knipe, David. *Hinduism*. San Francisco: HarperSanFrancisco, 1991.

Organ, Troy. *The Hindu Quest for the Perfection of Man*. Eugene, Or.: Wipf and Stock, 1998.

Isherwood, Christopher. *Vedanta for the Western World*. New York: Viking, 1973.

Islam

Haneef, Suzanne. *What Everyone Should Know About Islam and Muslims,* 12th edition. Chicago: Kazi Publishers, 1995.

Nasr, Seyyed Hossein. *Ideals and Realities of Islam*. New York: Frederick A. Praeger, 1967.

Judaism

Addison, Howard A. *The Enneagram and Kabbalah: Reading Your Soul*. Woodstock, Vt.: Jewish Lights, 1998.

Dosick, Wayne. *Living Judaism*. San Francisco: Harper-SanFrancisco, 1998.

———. *Soul Judaism*. Woodstock, Vt.: Jewish Lights, 1999.

Greenberg, Blu. *How to Run a Traditional Jewish Household*. New York: Simon & Schuster, 1983.

Kushner, Lawrence. *Honey from the Rock: An Introduction to Jewish Mysticism*. Woodstock, Vt.: Jewish Lights, 1999.

Siegel, Richard, Michael Strassfeld, and Sharon Strassfeld, eds. *The Jewish Catalog*. Philadelphia: Jewish Publication Society, 1973.

SPIRITUAL GUIDANCE

Barry, William & William Connolly. *The Practice of Spiritual Direction*. New York: Seabury, 1982.

Bawa Muhaiyaddeen. *Sheikh and Disciple*. Philadelphia: Bawa Muhaiyaddeen Fellowship, 1983.

Byrne, Lavinia, I.B.U.M., ed. *Traditions of Spiritual Guidance*. Collegeville, Minn.: Liturgical Press, 1990.

Dougherty, Rose Mary. *Group Spiritual Direction: Community for Discernment*. Mahwah, N.J.: Paulist Press, 1995. (Video also available through Paulist Press.)

Edwards, Tilden. *Spiritual Friend*. Mahwah, N.J.: Paulist Press, 1980.

Gratton, Carolyn. *The Art of Spiritual Guidance*. New York: Crossroad, 1992.

May, Gerald. *Care of Mind/Care of Spirit: Psychiatric Dimensions of Spiritual Guidance*. San Francisco: HarperSanFrancisco, 1992.

Merton, Thomas. *Spiritual Direction & Meditation*. Collegeville, Minn.: Liturgical Press, 1960.

Nemeck, F. K., and M. T. Coombs. *The Way of Spiritual Direction*. Wilmington, Del.: Michael Glazier Press, 1985.

Ochs, Carol & Olitzky, Kerry. *Jewish Spiritual Guidance*. San Francisco: Jossey-Bass, 1997.

Notes

Notes

Notes

Notes

Children's Spirituality

Becoming Me: *A Story of Creation*
by *Martin Boroson*
Full-color illus. by *Christopher Gilvan-Cartwright*

For ages 4 & up

NONDENOMINATIONAL, NONSECTARIAN

Told in the personal "voice" of the Creator, here is a story about creation and relationship that is about each one of us. In simple words and with radiant illustrations, the Creator tells an intimate story about love, about friendship and playing, about our world—and about ourselves. And with each turn of the page, we're reminded that we just might be closer to our Creator than we think!

8 x 10, 32 pp, Full-color illus., HC, ISBN 1-893361-11-X **$16.95**

A Prayer for the Earth
The Story of Naamah, Noah's Wife   AWARD WINNER!
by *Sandy Eisenberg Sasso*
Full-color illus. by *Bethanne Andersen*

For ages 4 & up

NONDENOMINATIONAL, NONSECTARIAN

This new story, based on an ancient text, opens readers' religious imaginations to new ideas about the well-known story of the Flood. When God tells Noah to bring the animals of the world onto the ark, God also calls on Naamah, Noah's wife, to save each plant on Earth. "A lovely tale. . . . Children of all ages should be drawn to this parable for our times." —*Tomie dePaola*, artist/author of books for children
9 x 12, 32 pp, HC, Full-color illus., ISBN 1-879045-60-5 **$16.95**

The 11th Commandment
Wisdom from Our Children   AWARD WINNER!
by The Children of America

For all ages

MULTICULTURAL, NONDENOMINATIONAL, NONSECTARIAN

"If there were an Eleventh Commandment, what would it be?" Children of many religious denominations across America answer this question—in their own drawings and words. "A rare book of spiritual celebration for all people, of all ages, for all time."—*Bookviews*
8 x 10, 48 pp, HC, Full-color illus., ISBN 1-879045-46-X **$16.95**

Children's Spirituality

In Our Image
God's First Creatures AWARD WINNER!

For ages 4 & up

by *Nancy Sohn Swartz*

Full-color illus. by *Melanie Hall*

NONDENOMINATIONAL, NONSECTARIAN

A playful new twist on the Creation story—from the perspective of the animals. Celebrates the interconnectedness of nature and the harmony of all living things. "The vibrantly colored illustrations nearly leap off the page in this delightful interpretation." —*School Library Journal*

"A message all children should hear, presented in words and pictures that children will find irresistible." —*Rabbi Harold Kushner*, author of *When Bad Things Happen to Good People*

9 x 12, 32 pp, HC, Full-color illus., ISBN 1-879045-99-0 **$16.95**

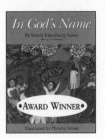

God's Paintbrush

For ages 4 & up

by *Sandy Eisenberg Sasso*; Full-color illus. by *Annette Compton*

MULTICULTURAL, NONDENOMINATIONAL, NONSECTARIAN AWARD WINNER!

Invites children of all faiths and backgrounds to encounter God openly in their own lives. Wonderfully interactive; provides questions adult and child can explore together at the end of each episode. "An excellent way to honor the imaginative breadth and depth of the spiritual life of the young." —*Dr. Robert Coles*, Harvard University

11 x 8½, 32 pp, HC, Full-color illus., ISBN 1-879045-22-2 **$16.95**

Also available: **A Teacher's Guide: *A Guide for Jewish & Christian Educators and Parents***
8½ x 11, 32 pp, PB, ISBN 1-879045-57-5 **$6.95**

God's Paintbrush Celebration Kit 9½ x 12, HC, Includes 5 sessions/40 full-color Activity Sheets and Teacher Folder with complete instructions, ISBN 1-58023-050-4 **$21.95**

In God's Name

For ages 4 & up

by *Sandy Eisenberg Sasso*; Full-color illus. by *Phoebe Stone*

MULTICULTURAL, NONDENOMINATIONAL, NONSECTARIAN AWARD WINNER!

Like an ancient myth in its poetic text and vibrant illustrations, this award-winning modern fable about the search for God's name celebrates the diversity and, at the same time, the unity of all the people of the world. "What a lovely, healing book!" —*Madeleine L'Engle*

9 x 12, 32 pp, HC, Full-color illus., ISBN 1-879045-26-5 **$16.95**

What Is God's Name? (A Board Book)

For ages 0–4

An abridged board book version of the award-winning *In God's Name*.

5 x 5, 24 pp, Board, Full-color illus., ISBN 1-893361-10-1 **$7.95**

Children's Spirituality

God Said Amen
by *Sandy Eisenberg Sasso*
Full-color illus. by *Avi Katz*

For ages 4 & up

MULTICULTURAL, NONDENOMINATIONAL, NONSECTARIAN

A warm and inspiring tale of two kingdoms: Midnight Kingdom is overflowing with water but has no oil to light its lamps; Desert Kingdom is blessed with oil but has no water to grow its gardens. The kingdoms' rulers ask God for help but are too stubborn to ask each other. It takes a minstrel, a pair of royal riding-birds and their young keepers, and a simple act of kindness to show that they need only reach out to each other to find God's answer to their prayers.

9 x 12, 32 pp, HC, Full-color illus., ISBN 1-58023-080-6 **$16.95**

For Heaven's Sake
by *Sandy Eisenberg Sasso*; Full-color illus. by *Kathryn Kunz Finney*

For ages 4 & up

MULTICULTURAL, NONDENOMINATIONAL, NONSECTARIAN

Everyone talked about heaven: "Thank heavens." "Heaven forbid." "For heaven's sake, Isaiah." But no one would say what heaven was or how to find it. So Isaiah decides to find out, by seeking answers from many different people. "This book is a reminder of how well Sandy Sasso knows the minds of children. But it may surprise—and delight—readers to find how well she knows us grown-ups too." —*Maria Harris*, National Consultant in Religious Education, and author of *Teaching and Religious Imagination*

9 x 12, 32 pp, HC, Full-color illus., ISBN 1-58023-054-7 **$16.95**

But God Remembered: Stories of Women from Creation to the Promised Land
by *Sandy Eisenberg Sasso*; Full-color illus. by *Bethanne Andersen*

For ages 8 & up

NONDENOMINATIONAL, NONSECTARIAN   AWARD WINNER!

A fascinating collection of four different stories of women only briefly mentioned in biblical tradition and religious texts. Award-winning author Sasso vibrantly brings to life courageous and strong women from ancient tradition; all teach important values through their actions and faith. "Exquisite. . . . A book of beauty, strength and spirituality." —*Association of Bible Teachers*   9 x 12, 32 pp, HC, Full-color illus., ISBN 1-879045-43-5 **$16.95**

God in Between
by *Sandy Eisenberg Sasso*; Full-color illus. by *Sally Sweetland*

For ages 4 & up

MULTICULTURAL, NONDENOMINATIONAL, NONSECTARIAN   AWARD WINNER!

If you wanted to find God, where would you look? A magical, mythical tale that teaches that God can be found where we are: within all of us and the relationships between us. "This happy and wondrous book takes our children on a sweet and holy journey into God's presence." —*Rabbi Wayne Dosick, Ph.D.*, author of *Golden Rules* and *Soul Judaism*

9 x 12, 32 pp, HC, Full-color illus., ISBN 1-879045-86-9 **$16.95**